THE RINEHART FRAMES

African
POETRY
BOOK SERIES

THE RINEHART FRAMES

Cheswayo Mphanza

Foreword by Kwame Dawes

University of Nebraska Press / Lincoln

Acknowledgments for the use of copyrighted
material appear on page 95, which constitutes
an extension of the copyright page.

The African Poetry Book Series has been made
possible through the generosity of philanthropists
Laura and Robert F. X. Sillerman, whose
contributions have facilitated the establishment
and operation of the African Poetry Book Fund.

Library of Congress Cataloging-in-Publication Data
Names: Mphanza, Cheswayo, author. | Dawes,
Kwame Senu Neville, 1962– writer of foreword.
Title: The Rinehart frames / Cheswayo
Mphanza; foreword by Kwame Dawes.
Description: Lincoln: University of Nebraska
Press, [2021] | Series: African poetry book series
Identifiers: LCCN 2020047082
ISBN 9781496225764 (paperback)
ISBN 9781496225818 (epub)
ISBN 9781496225825 (mobi)
ISBN 9781496225832 (pdf)
Subjects: LCGFT: Poetry.
Classification: LCC PS3613.P43 R56
2021 | DDC 811/.6—dc23
LC record available at
https://lccn.loc.gov/2020047082

Set and designed in Garamond Premier by N. Putens.

for Maunda Phiri and Nkhope Mphanza

zikomo pa vonse

I came into this world anxious to uncover the meaning of
things, my soul desirous to be at the origin of the world,
and here I am an object among other objects.
—FRANTZ FANON, *Black Skin, White Masks*

It appears as a revelation, as a momentary, passionate wish to grasp
intuitively and at a stroke *all* the laws of this world—its beauty and
ugliness, its compassion and cruelty, its infinity and its limitations.
—ANDREI TARKOVSKY, *Sculpting in Time*

CONTENTS

FOREWORD

KWAME DAWES

In one of the most memorable and moving sequences of his collection *The Rinehart Frames*, Zambian American poet Cheswayo Mphanza enacts an embodiment of a man from deep in the past of African history whose meaning to the struggle against colonialism, and the cost of resistance to Western colonialism, has become central to the myths, legends, and core ideological framings of this struggle:

> By slipping into the snug position of the casket, I finally understood the idiom "flirting with death" and the absurdity of calling myself human. I felt the appropriate scars I placed on my body: hacksaw marks like a collar around my neck and faux bullet holes I imagined deepened by the same sulfuric acid that left ant tunnels cutting through Lumumba's bones. Here I was as a body to contain Lumumba as myth and certainty. To resurrect him from an unknowable burial. At the start of the wake, I could feel Pauline's face staring hard, her tears streaming. I tried not to move, tasting salt in her tears. I wanted to speak to her as Lumumba. Tell her I had fabricated a letter on the lavender handkerchief stuffed in my front shirt pocket.

It is an elegant passage, imaginative in its invention as it constructs a scenario in which the body of Lumumba, desecrated by violence and the erasure caused by the use of acid by Lumumba's assassins, is somehow reimagined as a body in the poem "Open Casket Body Double for Patrice Lumumba's Funeral." In the poem, and in the title, one slowly recognizes that Mphanza is evoking other funereal instances filled with protest and the possibilities of resistance. His poem echoes the work of Gwendolyn Brooks writing about Emmett Till and other such historical elegies. Mphanza returns to Lumumba a few other times in the collection, and it is telling that the poet constantly finds himself employing a lyric mode to offer challenging elegies for many historical figures throughout this collection. In the poem "Djibril Diop Mambéty's Scene Descriptions," he presents a carefully staged moment in Lumumba's life, after "rotating stills" of Mugabe, Compoaré, Paul Biya, Idi Amin, and Bokassa:

> CUT TO: STOCK FOOTAGE. Camera unfolds to a crane view of Lumumba unboarding a plane with handcuffs on his wrists before rope is further tied around his arms. Mobotu in the background. His stare into the camera, an anthem collapsing.

In his poem "At David Livingstone's Statue," the speaker reflects on the legacy of certain names retained all over Africa even after the demise of colonialism. This encounter with residual wounds from the incursion of Europeans into Africa, an encounter characterized by a systematic erasure of identity, Mphanza invokes the lost names, the names abused by Western accounts of history, and in so doing he wrestles to un-silence these silences, not with dogma but with a moving lyric sensibility:

> It's the same sadness I carry when I think of Lumumba's
> exhumed and dissolved body. Pauline left to mourn
> the imagination of him—
>
> locating a compass of wounds. Our absence as fitting
> effigies for caskets.

Contained in these moments in which Lumumba is evoked is the achievement of Cheswayo Mphanza's ambitious collection of verse. Mphanza brings a distinctive sense of entitlement, not in the self-serving and self-indulgent manner that we have come to apply the term these days but in the way of someone who understands himself to be the inheritor of a rich and varied history and culture. Mphanza has created a series of "frames" that, based on his suggestion that the idea for them derives from his "reading" of the beautiful, but often violent, film *24 Frames*, by the late Iranian filmmaker Abbas Kiarostami, are best read as a carefully designed series that recreates the "historical moment" by imaginatively animating the "before" and "after" narratives framing the still moment, each account achieving a self-contained emotional power and intention, and yet when apprehended together, form a sophisticated cinematic composition.

Mphanza, in various moments in this book, describes these poems as centos. This, for an editor, introduces significant challenges and raises questions of attribution in a culture sensitive to copyright issues and issues of ownership but one in which, at the same time, access to information has been facilitated by the internet. After several exchanges with the poet, I came to recognize that the term *cento* is employed in both literal and metaphorical ways, and Mphanza's use of the form emerges from his intense sense of generosity and gratitude to the many scholarly and artistic influences that trigger much of the work.

To be sure, the book is filled with extensive quotes from multiple sources—poetic, fictional, historical, and scientific. In several of the early frames, the works are faithful centos, made up entirely of phrases and sentences found in the works of other writers. They are organized in the way a collagist would assemble ideas, colors, and shapes from scraps of fabric. Unlike the collagist, however, Mphanza does not seek to transform the quoted material but to retain its shape, its alienness, and to ensure that in many ways the tracing of its many paths of meaning can allow for a different kind of orchestration for each reader. But Mphanza, with the inclusion of attributing notes at the end of the work, draws attention to the form he has employed. The centos emerge here, then, as a physical enactment of a spirit of intellectual generosity and gratitude. Reading his work through this metaphorical lens is extremely fruitful, for what we are witnessing in this performance is an African writer footnoting his own intellectual history—showing that the postmodern Africa is shaped by colonialism, imperialism, traditionalism, and ideas and thoughts that straddle art, science, and the complicated history of migration and alienation of the African immigrant in the Western world. But the story of this poet is not the core theme—this is not Kamau Brathwaite's "harborless spade" with his belly of blues but a poet confident enough to announce the many ideas that he is engaging without feeling as if he is compromising his art and imagination.

There are centos in the collection, but there is much more when it comes to formal innovation: persona poems, lyric poems, songs, protest poetry, and much else. I cannot praise enough the possibilities that Mphanza introduces to us with this collection. At the same time, I believe that it is important for readers to come to this work with a mind to engage with what is on the page and with an openness to follow the trails the work creates to other sources of knowledge outside of the confines of the book.

One discovers quickly that Mphanza's ideas are not based on superficial engagements with information, or to put it more crudely, his ideas do not stop at the extended Wikipedia entry. Mphanza goes deeper. He investigates counter-narratives and counter-histories and explores ideas that are part of sometimes quite esoteric discussions about "settled" historical ideas. And he has done this while writing poems that are sensual and engaged in his own personal narrative of family, love, intellect, and the complexity of living as a Black man in America. In the end, I asked Mphanza to do what he could to grant attribution to the many lines that he samples in the poems, whether the sampling is direct quoting or a distorted layering of these voices. The notes represent an eclectic and exciting "guest list" for the gathering of voices and influences employed in this edifice. I return, then, to the metaphor of the gathering of "witnesses," and the list would include, randomly, Margaret Phiri (Mphanza's grandmother), Cornelius Eady, Édouard Glissant, Krzysztof Fijalkowski, Suzanne Césaire, Lester Young, Miles Davis, Gwendolyn Brooks, Vivan Sundaram, Brigit Pegeen Kelly, Amiri Baraka, Abdellatif Laâbi, Wallace Stevens, and dozens of others.

Yet while I would not describe the vast majority of these poems as centos, as is clear from his detailed notes at the end of the collection, Mphanza quotes and samples extensively in all the work we see collected here. There is, indeed, a need to be upfront about this here because poetry is a literary form that has thrived on the line, on the small moments of phrases and turns of phrases that are resonant with meaning and that often can function as synecdoche to the work and life of the writer. What I mean is that a brilliant line is often one of the persistent markers of the quality of a great poet. Mphanza, as with any gifted writer, knows a good line, a resonant line, an evocative line when he sees one, and as a result the unsuspecting may grant him credit, not for his taste (which is impeccable) but for the originality of his language. This is the risk that Mphanza takes, and what my many readings of this work has confirmed for me is that Mphanza's creative force lies in the way he creates rich and original composition by using a complex array of materials taken from various other creators. But it should be pointed out that Mphanza also composes his own "original" lines of beauty and skill.

As Mphanza explains in his notes at the end of the work, his centos are not strictly formed in that he does take some liberties with parts of speech and tense and other mechanics of the work he is quoting to fit into the fabric he is stitching together. And this stitching (I am now employing a related metaphor—the quilt) requires a gift for creating from a patchwork of words and phrases a coherent stretch of sentences that have clear meaning—a meaning that in the end belongs to the writer. Philosophically, one could argue that the cento is merely one step removed from the basic tenets of language and composition. The poet who is writing the conventional poem is said to be stitching together sentences with the use of words that exist and are available to her as part of the rich palette of language in her culture and her tradition. Julia Kristeva's term "intertextuality" comes to mind here, though the limits of this term should be acknowledged. The cento, it might well be argued, moves a step forward and presents the sentence, the phrase, and the paragraph as existing constructs available to the composer of ideas and thoughts. In this argument, of course, the ideas are flirting with, and troubling notions of, creativity, originality, appropriation, and copyright. Writers are likely to have mixed feelings about the function and practice of the cento, but one would be hard-pressed to deny the original invention found in the elaborate orchestration of ideas and language that is at work in *The Rinehart Frames*.

A week ago, the remarkable University of Nebraska Press design team, led in this instance by Nathan Putens, who has designed almost all the covers of African Poetry Book Foundation publications with UNP, sent me some mock-ups of covers for *The Rinehart Frames*. The image was striking and strangely familiar, although I could not immediately place its creator. It was a plate that was marked by a black cutout of a human figure in mid-motion, dressed in garments that suggested a different century, and dragging (a la *Mother Courage*) a stylized geometric compass, the kind used in cartography. Yet it was the background image that struck me as the dominant conception—an ancient-looking map of France framed by the Ocean Atlantique and the Mer

Cantabrique (The Sea of Cantabria). Putens offered some information about the artist, and then I recognized the work. It was the work of the brilliant South African artist William Kentridge.

As should be obvious, the image did not become the cover of this book, but the discussion about the use of the image was illuminating and speaks to what rests at the heart of Mphanza's lively and restless intellectual and artistic project. Mphanza had included Kentridge's art (and this image) in his responses to the questionnaire sent out to authors by UNP, as work that he thought spoke well to his project in the book. In his email to me about the choice, he wrote,

> My reasoning for the Kentridge piece, from the Porter Series, was because I had the chance to view Kentridge's work in Cape Town at a museum. The museum was showcasing his life's work in a series called "Why Must I Hesitate?" For me, this specific image I believe was the visual representation of *The Rinehart Frames* because it gets to the matter of the violence of geography. The Black body itself becoming a physical instrument on which to measure humanity, or lack thereof. And there is something in that amiability in how the Black body has been wielded into forms fitting whatever needs, wants, desires, etc., which speak to the ubiquitous nature in which *The Rinehart Frames* explores Blackness.

Here we understand right away Mphanza's ideological clarity and confidence. It is the kind of confidence that allows him to recognize in the work of an artist like Kentridge a certain affinity to anti-colonial practices and ideas. Yet even as Mphanza speaks to the work by Kentridge, we see how he employs his referential approach to construct a new poetics of resistance, even when the language is drawn from work that is, at the very least, problematic in its "use" of the Black body. I left our conversation impressed by Mphanza's approach, his poetics, and his generosity. And tellingly, the discussion, like my reading of this collection, took me deep into the work of Kentridge, in rewarding and fruitful ways. One imagines that for every artist, poet, historian, theorist, philosopher, and musician that Mphanza engages in this work, there are many more who he has had to leave out or who he has forgotten to acknowledge in some direct way. In this, Mphanza is not extraordinary. Much of the art we create is wisely read as derivative, as shaped by the ways we sample the voices that have formed us.

But what *The Rinehart Frames* does is to foreground this dynamic, and in so doing, one has the sense of being taken on a journey that could be called, "The Autobiography of the Sensibility of Cheswayo Mphanza."

For all the possibilities afforded to us in reading this work entirely through the formal prism of the cento, it is fair to say that Mphanza signals for the reader other ways to engage the work. From the opening frame, Mphanza introduces the Ralph Ellison trope of the dream/nightmare as a way to find meaning in the complex "reality" before us. Often, when a work that gestures toward the surreal or the magical—something fantastical, if you will—the suggestion that it is all a dream becomes a well-worn trope full of the weightiness of the mysteriousness of dreams and the almost transcendental access to knowledge and understanding that is, in many cultures, ascribed to dreams. Yet in the most colloquial and banal employments of the evocation of dream, the effect is a strange relief, a deus ex machina to a work in which the disorientation and confusion that can come with the surreal is explained by the dream. In a dream, the argument goes, anything goes. In his first frame of a series of frames that form the metaphorical language for the architecture of the collection, Mphanza introduces the dream as a platform of meaning: "What began it all was the bright bone of a dream I could hardly hold," and in this he speaks in the familiar language of biblical prophets and poets of the Western canon for whom the dream is a gateway to weighty meaning, to the unmitigated truth. And for Mphanza, this "bone of a dream" is one over which he has limited authority. This opening signals that we are entering a journey that will allow for the inexplicable to sit side by side with the understood and revealed. It is a theme that he takes up later in the collection as he quotes Hayao Miyazaki in an epigraph for his poem, "Getting Lost with Hayao Miyazaki and Satoshi Kon": "Be careful. This may be a dream, but you can still lose your head." Yet I am most interested in the motif of journey and quest suggested by this language, by this opening.

Throughout the collection, various figures come up for great scrutiny and consideration, among them Lester Young, the troubled jazz great who, in the poem "Lester Leaps In," is positioned as a misogynistic alcoholic and drug addict whose desire for "cool" is pursued at the expense of the women in his life. Yet in that study, there is a capacity for tenderness and recognition that art can come with deep human costs in a society that is structured around racism and dehumanization—the nation symbolized in the Rinehart figure of Ellison's *Invisible Man* that forms the core motif and intellectual grounding of this work. Yet, it is in his treatment of his countryman, the late Henry Tayali, that we are given a splendid example of Mphanza's commitment to the reframing of Black art and Black identity through innovative poetic technique.

As ubiquitous as these innovations are in this collection, they never seem superfluous in their application. Indeed, a reading of his work, his notes, and his thoughts about the collection suggests restlessness of thought and active and persistent engagement with knowledge that he is trying to find a way to bring to bear on the poem. Indeed, the poem seems inadequate to the task, and so the work is marked by multiple allusions, references, footnotes, internal quotations, and much more. The swirl of ideas and considerations around philosophy, history, and religion and theories ranging from Dadaism, postcolonialism, deconstructionism, Black nationalism, pan-Africanism lead to invention, ways to bring all of these to bear on the lyric impulse. His poem for Henry Tayali, "Notes toward a Biography of Henry Tayali," uses the Japanese storytelling practice Pecha Kucha. Here, Mphanza enacts a combination gallery installation, slideshow, and theatrical performance through reference to specific works of Tayali's art to explore the making of the artist, the complex and troubled journey of the evolution of this Zambian artist. The work's theatricality is found in Mphanza's decision to embody Tayali by speaking in the first person:

> This country does tether us. A cord pulled from the Zambezi River.
> Our birthright to our father's tribes, but we are always our mother's children.
> Bury me here when I inherit the still life of my woodcuts. Smear my ashes
> on the Nsalu Cave paintings. I am thinking of my father who adorned
> himself griot. I do not worry about legacy, let my art remain.

The Rinehart Frames is the eighth winner of the Sillerman First Book Prize in African Poetry, and it continues in the tradition of innovative and varied approaches to the practice of poetry by poets from Africa and her recent diaspora. Cheswayo's contribution to African poetry is consistent with the energy, daring, and risk of writers and artists who are being touted as the proponents of AfroFurturism. As with all labels and movements, this one has its own issues of definition and conceptualization, but at its most basic level, it seems to speak to a genuine inclination among African writers to push against both the imposed Western norms that form part of the legacy of colonialism and imperialism while at the same time recognizing a challenge to new and old orthodoxies in African literature, many developed in resistance to colonialism. We are given a chance to be guided into the future by artists who bring discipline, intelligence, and emotional alertness to their work, and Cheswayo Mphanza is certainly one of this cadre of poets emerging out of Africa today.

Frame One

And because I mean to live transparently, I am here, bear with me, describing the contents.
What began it all was the bright bone of a dream I could hardly hold.
The sky was gray, but the sun was making little silver promises:
a perturbation of the light;
the wind tilting slowly;
thin collars of fog;
autumn's mist pressed to ashes.
I stretched all senses.
I bended in peculiar angles—
a public breathing through the night.
Forgotten names sang through my head.
Names meant to conjure sultry nights.
I lingered a little to listen to the singing in my ears:
the perfect, the terror,
the musculature.
I was somehow attuned to it all
and I began to tremble so violently.
My tongue was difficult—
voice still, a well of dark water, a prayer.
My eyes grew dim and I could no more gaze—
I don't know what I'm becoming
that breaks what's left of what's human in me.

THE RINEHART FRAMES

/

The Code of Hammurabi

John Laing, "(Lenge)," Lusaka, Zambia

Reading Glissant makes
        me anxious
   of the body's properties.

      Our catachrestic error in
defining *being* as *human*.
          I can't help but to think

      of our existence as icterids—
the jaundiced ones. Take for instance
   the precarity of being witness

         to another's body: A man is caught
   stealing a bag of flour.
          Cornmeal dust and ash covering

     his skin. Dryness
   around his busted lips, bare feet.
        The flared ribs. His head

in the position of shame,
    shadowed by John Laing's statue
ahead. The rest of him penumbra.

      Hands tied behind his back
  with the same rope used
        to connect plows

between cows. Shirt stripped off
his back. Swollen bruises
mapping it. Two men at his side

dragging him to law. The gathered
crowd, even their shadows hostile,
scrambling for a part

of his body to wail against. My young eyes
resting on his back. So inanimate
the body is from a distance;

a well-stuffed scarecrow.
His spine perfect for my blow
before a kick to the back

of his knees, before my untrained
jab at his ribs. My fist
the size of a ripe tangerine. His pulsating

body a shock in my hands
to feel him
as a live thing.

Frame Two

I awoke ahead of myself—
the mind roamed as a moth roams.
Warm dusk had deepened into amorous darkness,
snow's echo, time raining down.
Night like so many such nights I've known.
I wept with bitter longing, not remembering how in my youth I cried.
To have had some joys and to tenderly recall them—
a way of breaking synchronistic through time—
being adrift in place.
Strange to see meanings that clung together once—
the rush of whole lives passing elsewhere without you.
How tragic the force of destiny can be;
how we squander our hours of pain;
how aspects of myself could be rendered.

Frame Three

The arterial clouds shouldered a glassy reservoir.
Pale morning light dying in shadows,
blue flames burning.
Confettied to shreds, the last leaves darken gusts.
The birds repeat a warning I think I should understand;
their lives the way stars hold to the sky.
I must have seen in them some measure of myself.
Everywhere the shadows of my voice
absurdly hammering a prelude of its own.
I listen and little by little I perceive that voice's harmony.
It makes a flute-like sound—
capricious monotone—
a sound like held breath escaping;
a cruel silence in the night.

Getting Lost with Hayao Miyazaki and Satoshi Kon

Be careful. This may be a dream, but you can still lose your head.
—Giovanni Battista Caproni to Jiro Horikoshi, *The Wind Rises* (Hayao Miyazaki, 2013)

It all happened so sudden, or has it always been happening?
The trigger from a woman's sight at the farmers' market
which sent me on an impulse inward into
the convex vestibules of memory. My wandering through
the past; all the endless doors marked "etc.," which felt like veiled entries into
tragic addendums of living. My pondering over what other ways can I speak
of the shadows of the past? Umbra makes them sound beautiful. Before I
attempt to speak, my mouth snatched from me, burning secrets the tongue
salivates over. An attempt to scream from the eyes,
but they only become witness to the trails of smoke
I chase to find the origin or departure of my journey.
How do I get back? Hitchhike the train swimming across water—
where passengers look like shades of me—or castles moving in the sky?
Sunflowers spilling from their sides; the wind sneezing a light breeze
to plant them in small valleys; perfect shades of blue and green
demarcating real from surreal. The shy ghosts and ghouls; monsters paid
to play minstrels of themselves; the boogeyman with a wife, kids, and a mortgage.
Be careful to dream too much—your imagination can destroy their homes.
Try existing as a guest wherever you are. Then I want to return to a place
I can believe in, but the imagination holds all my anxieties.
When life is moving so slow, it is trying to spit you into someplace
elsewhere. The life you know is camouflage. A voice or touch can appear
as a cruel phantom after being alone long enough—when I listen
to my breath to believe I am alive. *There are doors we could*
lead you to, but you must not mind the dead. Don't trust the ground.
Your body either. If anything, learn to mistrust yourself. Some
of what we remember becomes fragile with time until they become
constructions out of our own desires. Notice the tulips

smell like daffodils? The mind is projection—you ever think
our imagination intrudes upon other worlds? Our reality a fanatic's
crazed dreams? Consider we too might be someone's arid construction.
But if I succumb to the imagination's fold, will I have a song like
the Kauaʻi ʻōʻō to ricochet from its fantastical graveyard? To sear
my voice on time's ears? *Here is the way out. The destination is the same*
in that you are always arriving and departing part of you. Turn outward.
Where are you now, but where you have always been?

Frame Four

after *Playtime* (Jacques Tati, 1967)

The crawling day arrives on skinned knees
and the whole bedazzled city's an arcade. Magnificent
sky like the inside of a skillet and bright as ghosts.
Warm as my face,
a golden light hails me.
Sun out like a floodlight.
In the old melancholy park, leaves spin out of autumn.
The ribs of leaves lie in the dust
before ash filigrees roses carved in the wood of weeping trees.
To tempt our hands,
whole beds of bloom pitched on a pile
leave fingers brushed with yellow pollen.
Astonishing in their suddenness, their quietude, their wetness.
I saw the sprouts and plants growing through light and then darkness.
Light coughs in the bushes—
too green the springing April grass.
A small bird sings in shadows,
chirping swallows slip, dripping down through the roof of spring.
Dancing blue images, shades of blue pasts
pinned into air, stuck in time.
Something like smoke rises from the snuffed-out distance.
A silver tear, a tiny flame—
sounds of water pouring.
Shadows cast shadows ad infinitum—
a mysterious blur to a soft sinister glowing.

Looking to the sky, hoping it will bleed light,
a silence grows too loud to ignore.
Silence that structures a voice in the dark.
The sudden arpeggios of laughter lilting across—
voices soft in the mellow dusk;
the slight rub of untongued voices—
everything was fortissimo.
The decorous walking around me, sounds of footsteps—
hobbles in the red wind.
I mount the scabbed streets, the long shouts of avenues,
and in the interval between familiar faces, events occurred:
the train sped by with its cargo of light;
I saw a street sweeper praying, pressing his forehead on a melon rind;
traffic stalls to bricks shattering.
I walk closer to the traffic's noise—
the driver longing for death;
storefront churches asking for mercy;
damp, wet bricks and stones, clean bones of daylight.
A crack in the wall fights the persistent advances of the sunlight.
One child runs past, stops, and bends down to secure his loose shoelace;
old men fighting death in secret corners,
the rain-wet alleys.
Someone grieves or weaves, counts or sings—
a fawn figure with a filigreed grin—
a long breath singer.
Humans in darkness and in light.
Someone whispering into someone's ear, someone crying behind a door
and I am not that far away.

Lester Leaps In

I bet Prez thinks he is heroin cool,
        floating on the thin, sinking
                sheets of ice in a crisp drink

icing his veins. He must think
        he knows how to speak tongues
           with one furl

of his sopping lips
        sucking the gold-toothed
                and parched mouth

of another woman who heard
        him play, but was oblivious
                to the malice surging.

He probably picked her up
        with a line about how a woman's body
           is like a saxophone,

caressing her waist with the
        weighted history in his
                rigid palms, running

chilled fingers down her spine,
    reaching for keys in her ribs,
        pressing until she sounded

like bebop. Who could love a mouth
    loaded with unabridged languages
        resonating in the residues

of his gums? The burgeoning plaque
    and funk of not giving a fuck
        one too many times;

the stifling cavities acquired from numbing
    the mouth with the coolness
        of coke. I wonder

where he finds air after spoiling
    his lungs with a frozen and thawing
        drink, muddy like brandy

with its drying burn, or ancient
    like gin, what my mama calls:
        the deadbeats-no-good-two-

timing-ass-nigger's-drink-of-choice.
    Prez, a prisoner of cool, pities those
        who have tried drinking

from both glasses—my father.
    Moonshine mouth-scented,
        stumbles home over my mother,

with her own platinum-toothed
    and thirst-ridden mouth
        from a brisk drink.

My father breathlessly whispers: *Baby,*
   you are some kind of instrument—
      blindly looking for the keys

in her ribs, when they could've been strings
   or woodwind tone holes, so unaware
      of what sounds she makes.

I stare at my father, my voice
   restraining a hoarseness
      hissing my disdain. How uncool

and unlearned his frigid fingers,
   unable to locate where the body
      needs to be pressed,

plucked, or gently tapped. His fear
   of the sinking sheets of ice
      in a cold drink

the only time he can conquer cool
   when he shrinks in himself, unable
      to hear the music of her body.

II

Frame Five

I am black within as is this skin.
My body a heavy meat on bones.
        I must be responsible for it.
I have been many things in this life.
             Too often not having proof of myself.
I know there is a person composed of my parts,
      a sleeve of light,
a radiance inside of time,
        an assurance.

Frame Six

These days I wake in the used light of someone's spent life.
I am often a stranger to myself;
I have no place of origin, no home.
I keep remembering everything in two time zones at once.
Who knows, maybe I myself am called something other than myself.
Not so much a name, but the result of a name.
It's a strange sensation to yell out: *this is me!*
In every place I've watched caravans of sorrow—
I run like all the other men, chasing my shadow down alleys.
Sometimes in the spaces, there is fear—
my mind deepens into them.
From calm to fear my mind moves, then *moves*—
in light part nightmare and part vision fleeing.
The voice rises on a storm of grackles, then returns—half elegy, half serenade.

Open Casket Body Double for Patrice Lumumba's Funeral

By slipping into the snug position of the casket, I finally understood the idiom "flirting with death" and the absurdity of calling myself human. I felt the appropriate scars I placed on my body: hacksaw marks like a collar around my neck and faux bullet holes I imagined deepened by the same sulfuric acid that left ant tunnels cutting through Lumumba's bones. Here I was as a body to contain Lumumba as myth and certainty. To resurrect him from an unknowable burial. At the start of the wake, I could feel Pauline's face staring hard, her tears streaming. I tried not to move, tasting salt in her tears. I wanted to speak to her as Lumumba. Tell her I had fabricated a letter on the lavender handkerchief stuffed in my front shirt pocket. And how it made me think of the manila envelope I kept a manuscript of poems in labeled: *freedom papers*. I wanted to tell Pauline I knew of her bare-breasted march in Leopoldville. The death of our daughter I was not allowed to mourn. Breaking protocol, I whispered in Pauline's ear to read my handkerchief. To ignore its stains, but to bear the contents smudged in silk. That is when Pauline lay her hands on my face, bent her body over, and wailed. How then could I resist holding her?

My beloved companion:

> *I write you these words not knowing whether you will receive them, when you will receive them, and whether I will still be alive when you read them. The snapdragon flowers I picked out for you should have come as an omen when I saw how their seedpods look like skulls. I write to you from the great beyond, Pauline. This letter a small excerpt of my heart. You never knew about that night in Katanga. No one was to know of the firing squad, the axes gnashing through cartilage, cracking like drywood, and the acidic bath to dissolve me. Foolish me who thought this body was not ephemeral for the Belgians. How I never*

learned to compromise with this existence as internecine. I write to you thinking of our youth. The tenderness that grips me when I helped put on your earrings. Young lovers bruising each other's necks with kisses. Here I was thinking I was a monolith in the world. Then in stumbles you reducing me to my most ordinary. Our promenading in Kinshasa as Évolués, me selling bottles of La Polar in one hand and years later drafting Loi Fondamentale. The drowned-out echoes of our promises for this country. Its right to an honorable life, to perfect dignity, to independence with no restrictions. The irreparable debt we will forever be owed. Yes, I, too, made mistakes. The privations of my love I, at times, kept from you. Which helped me understand what makes a man a dictator is the same as his need for freedom. A facsimile of that which has conquered him. I want our children, whom I leave behind, to be told that the future of the Congo is beautiful. All of these things I can't shake free. Like who will water the garden, grease Juliene's scalp, and braid her hair into pigtails with neon pearls dangling. Do not weep for me, my companion. History will have its day one day.

Notes toward a Biography of Henry Tayali

A Pecha Kucha

[*The Village*. Silkscreen Print.]

I was born with a language seared on my tongue. I sipped from
my father's bottle of pale ale as he rocked me to sleep. I have
starved a mad dog until it could learn to kneel to me. I have held
a chicken down before my grandmother cleaved its neck clean.
I ate its body whole, sometimes chewing the bones.

[*Bull*. Scrap Metal.]

Our summer of love at Victoria Falls. Zamrock the culprit.
Bodies whirling to Paul Ngozi. In the gyre of apartheid farther
south and being over the edge of independence. What was
freedom if not our bodies thrust from ourselves and we
trying to catch them in our arrested dances?

[*Regina in My Dreams*. Stencil Sketch.]

I pull a petal off a Blue Curiosa. You blossom from its
edges. Bees gossiping around you. The rattle in your legs,
a barefooted dance in white sand. A child's delicate step
on his mother's back. I want to learn to pronounce your
body—fold your name at the back of my mouth.

[*Untitled*. Oil on Hardboard.]

The canvas begins with no paint or name attached. I go back
to my birth in Serenje by the Nsalu Caves. When Zambia was
Northern Rhodesia. My wails winnowed like Wilson's snipe.
The scene where my father held me as if I was artifact. Rooms
that coated us into primary colors as we tugged against our skin.

[*Herd Boy*. Scrap Metal.]

The West was calling my name. Kaunda's dream to show the
African has imagination. I longed for Paris or Florence but settled
for Germany at Staatliche Kunstakademie Düsseldorf. I learned
their language. Read and studied their canon—from Caspar David
Friedrich to Adolph von Menzel—enough to anoint me civilized.

[*People in the Summer*. Oil on Canvas.]

At the touch of a paintbrush, or chisel, before I approached the
canvas, block of wood, or scrap metal, my anxiety was that I
saw the body as Western. I was trying to get away from myself
so I turned to the abstract. The splotches of color coated
bodies to hide beggars, huts, villages, and the African.

[*Unfinished Self-Portrait with Brother Bright Tayali*. Stencil Sketch.]

We grind our bodies on the rise. Lick last night's fog from our
lips. Rub the cruel visions captured from our eyes and muzzle
our mouths until screams or swelling moans exhaust themselves.
Recycle the carnage into rage and the courage it needs to blossom;
the dismal loneliness required to live or leave this life.

[*The Other Side of the Bar*. Woodcut.]

Sometimes the night is generous and I don't drown as much.
Enough munkoyo courses through me. A drop more and I
pass over to the other side where I become pantomime for my
body strung out at the corner of the bar. Silence subdues me.
Listen: I want to leave this country something other than my body.

[*Attempt at an Abstract Painting*. Oil on Canvas.]

I was trying to understand my country in the erasure. Women
whose features I did not define and left as polka dots with
head wraps or chitenges around their waists. Was it shame
that defined me, hiding in the edges of my art to make room
for universal appeal? To be regarded as an artist erased of race?

[*A Measure of Cooking Oil*. Woodcut.]

Is modernity shedding ourselves to become exotic fixtures upon lips
of Western critics? *I remain a son of my country. I am a fragment of it.*
A particle. My art is concerned with the suffering of the people. I want
it to be the echo of that suffering. I see the problems of the continent. I am
recording what I and my people feel, but I do not attempt to provide answers.

[*Leica SLR Negative Filmstrips.*]

A child eating cassava. Regina's twisted mouth, cursing me in a
mixture of Nyanja, Bemba, and Tonga. David Livingstone's statue.
Regina dancing with a white cloth in her left hand. A man burning
a kwacha note. A plate of nshima and kapenta. Lusaka at night,
littered in variations of light splotches and dark voids.

[*The Beggar*. Woodcut.]

I was thinking of the man I saw in Kitwe, resting at the side of a dirt
road. He reached his hands to the sky, pretending to fluff one of the
clouds before sleeping. Maybe he dreamed about finding a country.
One not landlocked. His hands outstretched to reach his people.
Each of them singing in varied tones of an insatiable hunger.

[*Destiny*. Oil on Canvas.]

Realism attempts to render the truth while expressionism is a bad
liar who wants to be honest. This was where I found myself when my
dream of *Destiny* awoke me. It needed to come from the excavated
land I saw Zambia becoming. I took red soil, mixed it with oil, and
and threw away my watercolors—my fear of their dilution of me.

[*Huts*. Silkscreen Print.]

The straw spires send me back to running through fields, brushing
against corn husks. The smell of hollow clay rooms, food laid on mats,
the water-bowl we passed to wash our hands. Firewood burning in a
small enclosure. Its blue flames we held all July where we saw winter
pass with a thief's caution, stealing what remained of our warmth.

[*Untitled.* Woodcut.]

I see three contours of Regina. All of them the woman I loved and
lost. Gina, is it not you I see in the woodcuts I chisel into effigies?
Their backs shaped like kandolos. Your face, Zambia's best export—
copper. In the mind, I seesaw from the living to your grave. What I'd
give to peel the afterlife's underside to see you under life's awning.

[*Pounding Maize.* Woodcut.]

I keep a picture of my mother pounding maize in my front shirt
pocket. Photography is best for its simple truth: thought is brief,
whereas the image is absolute. This is how I want to remember her:
the care in the handle of the falling log; my clinging to her back
wrapped in a chitenge; and her movements lulling me to sleep.

[*Lusaka Burning.* Stencil Sketch.]

Birds in flight fleeing their nests. Flapping flames off wings. The
Zambezi River a shattered disco ball spitting out shards of crystallized
water. Zambia's language milieu where the word for pain is a shared
dialect. Nyanja is a fire language, crackling the mouth, and shearing
consonants off tongues. What is left is no country, but the imagination.

[*The Omen.* Watercolor.]

The moon started to fold into itself. Crows waking at dawn.
The revelation that stretched my life from star to star. The small
thread of a man's life and where he chose to plot and root
himself. If I were to weave that thread once more, I wish
for more scenes holding Regina, letting my art be background.

[*The Brothers.* Oil on Canvas.]

On a drive through Lusaka, W.I.T.C.H.'s tender vibrato holds
me. I know this country tethers us. We will all share the same death.
The phantom blood of the '80s, which moved our lives at the pace of
a stone in a child's hands upon view of open water. The scene that took
me back to reading by candlelight until the wick burned into itself.

[*Mother Afrika*. Woodcut.]

This country does tether us. A cord pulled from the Zambezi River.
Our birthright to our father's tribes, but we are always our mother's children.
Bury me here when I inherit the still life of my woodcuts. Smear my ashes
on the Nsalu Cave paintings. I am thinking of my father who adorned
himself griot. I do not worry about legacy, let my art remain.

III

Frame Seven (with Director's Commentary*)

for Ruchita Chandrashekar

Mouth that moved my mouth to song.
You who pluck consonants like silver from the generous air,
breath hanging overhead, a fever to the sky.
Your mouth recites a wordless vow;
your chamomile breath;
your deep-throated discourse—
the pressure of your exhale.
You take my breath
and your breath disappearing in my lungs.
I find my way by following your spine:
your kindling limbs, branches of extinguished blossoms.
Your hands find me where there is no science, only precision.
Your slight shifting;
your sorting, tearing, putting aside;
your way past your old hurts, crumbling like dust;
your own belated breath.
Some voyagers dream of you walking through their twisting lanes—
you are yourself another country.
You this world's blue thirst.
I want you as a tremor of dawn,
our day, serenaded by dust.
—you deny, you deny, you deny—
You swear sometimes I am your nemesis, even.
I am your dotage, your vulnerable season;
your sleeping form;
your vows of homecoming;
your secret passions into being.

---

*I am most humble in my humanity when I am in love. The repeated utterances or positioning of the "you" (love's anaphoric logic) become its alembics. Positioning the "you" as the cause and effect not of but on "I"; the "I" never selfishly present, only existing in relation to "you." Or the "I" becoming "your(s)." A profound human gratuity.

Taste of Cherry (Abbas Kiarostami, 1997)

On a drive with Mr. Badii in his tan Land Rover, silence grazes our ears, leaving our mouths half open, our throats letting out small clearings. The roads ahead wind into Möbius strips. Mr. Badii's hands loosely grabbing the wheel. I look to the Rover's tinted windows, wondering if we appear like Schrödinger's cat to other drivers, but I know it is the ostrich syndrome holding my silence when he asks me to pour twenty spadefuls of earth on his body in a hole he dug. On a street discreet as our intent, searching for Mr. Badii's perfect burial, the lakefront's scent curls around us, retreating me to sore summers. The tension I developed against water after a friend drowned. A pack of boys tightly bound as a tin of sardines. The soda cans in brown paper bags we carried to give us the mysticism of winos. Weight of Slaughter and Son Funeral Home sign tugging at our collars: [*A Death Has Occurred or is Near*]. The brown and orange liquid we poured on fish combed by waves to shorelines. Their bodies braised by seagull beaks, eyes sinking into their skulls. We stuffed half-lit loose cigarettes inside them so their musk would not offend our noses. "I don't want to give you a gun to kill me; I'm giving you a spade," Mr. Badii says. "Just pretend you're farming and I am manure to spread at the foot of crops." We reach a stoplight. My eyes expand to the bus that ran over the neighbor's daughter. The mother running to scattered limbs, attempting to sew back the severed child. I stared in wonder, thinking it was possible. "This city is a burial—why do you choose to live?"

Frame Eight

Although the world forgets me,
        tonight and all the nights to come
                I dare to speak of my darkness.
I cultivated myself where the sun gutters from the sky—
        my truths are all foreknown.
        I want clear days and nights and no secrets,
but also to invest the world with a clearer understanding of itself.
        I know what power inhabits me—
            this slight tickling, this light madness.
                            I am free of limitations.
        I know the general outline of despair,
            the web of the inner levels of the mind.
Every silent wailing could find its place in these acts.
                    The future contains nothing uncertain—
        I rejoice that things are as they are
for I have known them all already, known them all.
                          Everything has an instant in which it is:
        fragments of being; being or nothing; near not being.
The wheels of circumstance that grind so terribly within the mind,
                        the hurt this world could give.
  I am here eyes half-open clinging to the thread that sews day to night.
        I shall whisper heavenly labials in a world of gutturals;
            I will say nothing that I feel is a lie or unproven;
                I will have a voice, a color;
                  I will be a light thing.

Auteur Poetica

It is not description which can unveil the efficacy
and beauty of monuments, seas, or the human face
in all their maturity and native state, but rather
evocation, allusion, suggestion.
—Stéphane Mallarmé, "Crisis in Poetry"

    Considering modern poetry,
I look to my garden.
        Outside my window,

           the snout butterfly feasts
               on my flowers while
approaching the end of

its fortnight. Staining its wings
           with the pollen of perennials
and phlox. Not the butterfly's

           beauty I marvel at,
      but how it comprehends
    its dimming hours; the skill in living.

    The flowers
know something about this.
              How beauty is of dissonance

           to the sentimental. The poet's voice
           still and absent
        understanding the ethereal

nature of the line's breath.
　　　Its inconclusive possibilities—
　aside from our abuse

　　　　　　　of its frame and projections
　　　on the page, conflating
affect as synecdoche for craft.

　The poem is a pure thing.
　　　　　Each writer finds a new entrance
　　　into the mystery.

　　　　　Each line melody;
　　its strands concocting
　　　their own cadences—

　meaningful folds, slight tears
　　　　at the seams. How a line
　　can be naked without being explicit—

　　　　　We tore petals from monocots.
　　　　　Put them between our lips
　　　　　　　and pressed secrets into them—

　　　　　the imagists' wet dream.
　　　To build the voice
　　　　　as an individual instrument.

　　To fashion a new air
　　　where breath becomes superfluous.

Djibril Diop Mambéty's Scene Descriptions

We wanted freedom, but we got democracy.
—Hugh Masekela

Scene 1: ESTABLISHING SHOT. The scene must be like an intermittent dream, coming on then drifting. The camera's demand of austerity. Small incisions of light. A black blank screen. Ominous wails and chatter of Africans rising in the unknown background.

Scene 2: CLOSE UP. Rotating Stills. "The Upright Man" Thomas Sankara adorning a red beret. Kwame Nkrumah, Jomo Kenyatta. Sékou Touré. CUT TO: STOCK FOOTAGE of political propaganda. CUT TO: A ROLL and B ROLL of African liberation armies. Coups. Low-angle shots zooming into farms being salted. Townships and villages burning. Muddy puddles reflecting the fire. ZOOM OUT: A lush landscape of green. The sky a grainy sienna. CUT TO: Rotating stills of Robert Mugabe: Blaise Compaoré: Paul Biya: Idi Amin: Bokassa standing in front of his bold eagle-styled golden throne. CUT TO: STOCK FOOTAGE. Camera unfolds to a crane view of Lumumba unboarding a plane with handcuffs on his wrists before rope is further tied around his arms. Mobotu in the background. His stare into the camera, an anthem collapsing.

Scene 3: WIDE SHOT. Political cartoon of the scramble for Africa. CUT TO: Colonial map of Zambia, then known as Northern Rhodesia. Its edges show Angola bordering west. Democratic Republic of the Congo northwest. Tanzania northeast. Malawi east. Mozambique southeast. Namibia southwest. Zimbabwe and Botswana south.

Scene 4: A black blank screen with the sound of a train approaching in the background. FADE IN: Mining newspaper the *Nchanga Drum*. On its cover a map showing Northern Rhodesia's Copperbelt railroad line from Livingstone in the south to the Belgian Congo border. A photograph of white and African miners. Camera zooms into the picture. Entering. The photograph no longer a still setting. Bodies move. White arms and black arms holding pickaxes rise and break in unison against sacred rock. CUT TO: Mining train passing by miners. Zambian women holding their children at the side while selling grain.

Scene 5: CUTBACK: Colonial map of Northern Rhodesia. Kenneth Kaunda's frame growing on top. A litany of abbreviations cut across. ALC, ANC, UNIP, ZANC, ZNBC, UP, UPP, PAFMECSA, PLP, CAA, CAI, CAS, ANIP, AZ, FUCA, MMD, NAZ, UDI, CCMG.

Scene 6: STOCK FOOTAGE of Kaunda on a podium giving a speech at the University of Zambia. "It pays to belong to the UNIP! One Zambia, One Nation, One Country."

Scene 7: WIDE SHOT of Lusaka Independence Stadium. October 23–24, 1964. Zambia's army band playing. CUT TO: TIGHT SHOT of the Union Jack waving as it comes down. Zambia's flag ascends. Northern Rhodesia is no more. Zambia is born. Chants from the crowd of "One Zambia, One Nation, One Country!"

Scene 8: MEDIUM SHOT of Zambia's countryside. Morning mist where the trees are covered in smog. CUT TO: Zambezi River. CUT TO: WIDE SHOT of Victoria Falls, showing David Livingstone's statue in Zimbabwe. Dusk falls. FADE OUT.

Scene 9: CLOSE SHOT. The screen unfolds into color, showing a dim room. Two young lovers, both infants of freedom's spring, laying on a straw mattress bed facing a large flag covering the wall. (He doesn't know he has hung the flag backward). Her head resting on his dead arm. A window open, wind whipping at a loose screw on the side.

Scene 10: CUT TO outside the small room. Though the sky is crowded with storm clouds, the jack snipes don't stop singing. Their song is a lisp in the wind. The scene retracts back into black and white. CUT TO inside the room. Blocks of letters spelling out "C-O-P-P-E-R-B-E-L-T P-R-O-V-I-N-C-E." A plastic ornament of an African mask above the bedside table.

Scene 11: MEDIUM SHOT. Static showing on a wooden Zenith television set inside the room before a scene plays from Ousmane Sembène's *Xala* (1975): "Two white men carrying briefcases walk in on a congressional meeting held by African leaders dressed in Western attire. The African leaders clap at the president who resembles Léopold Senghor. He uses words such as 'revolutionary' and 'independence' and they garner an applause. The white men place briefcases in front of each leader. They open them and their eyes shine with green. The Léopold Senghor parody rises and announces, 'modernity must make us lose our Africanality.' They all clap and disappear with the briefcases into limousines. TV set goes off." Camera continues panning around the room of the young lovers. Fela Kuti and The Africa 70 album poster of *Confusion* next to Miriam Makeba's solitary stare, turning away from Fela. Facing Papa Wemba instead. (Unbeknownst to the boy, the girl knows something about geography. His abuse of the backward-hung flag.)

Scene 12: TIGHT SHOT. The camera elevates from the bottom of their bed to a parallel scale of the two. The girl reaches for a radio at bedside. Tuning in to Zambia National Broadcasting Corporation (ZNBC). Color reenters as Zamrock slowly seeps into the scene. Blackfoot's "Running" plays as their bodies become blurred naked under the stream of moonlight entering through the window. He kisses her belly button, calls it a compass, following its southernmost trail. He tells her "your skin is beautiful. How one might just mistake pollen for cinnamon." She lifts his head gently to her face and kisses him. She says, "I'm learning how to take care of flowers. To not worry about the carnations as much as the lilies." He wonders how much less he is in the dark. His mind still in Northern Rhodesia. Landlocked country. "God Save the Queen" still slides on his tongue when he speaks. She will say she used to belong to a nation, but it kept a record of her raptures so she dissolved it. The moonlight will shine brighter. Revealing parts of his body he wants clothed. He will think, "I must possess myself." She will ask what nation he belongs to? His answer, her body. A ruthless allegiance. To claim her as a country. Call her a nation. Carve a kiss on her collarbone and call it a flag. She will tell him independence exacerbates the abrasions of a country. To ask a nation why its flag bears red. The thought of freedom as an open wound. Silence could be useful if he knew its cadence. Maybe the fourth wall should be broken. To invite others into his discomfort. Or maybe they remain as is. Sinking back into bed where he learns making love is immigrating to someone. A citizen who feigns to be a refugee under the tender weight of skin and its nudging. The unpronounceable pleas of the mouth soaring into an anthem he imagines his. To sustain the borders of her body or coalesce the floor into deep country before they are lulled to sleep. His dream of a nation as suspended and ethereal as her weight next to his. Camera pulls away into a long shot, the focus blurs.

IV

Frame Nine

I invite you to a moment of truth;
> I can't say who I am unless you agree I'm real.
> I, too, am often misrecognized in the dark.
>> A dull head among windy spaces.
> I would like to believe in the reality of my body and its needs—
>> even its comforts are hideous uses I strain to understand.
>> All day my body accepts what it is—
>>> it is too much to bear sometimes.
> There is something in me so cruel, so silent—
>> something dark, lustful, dangerous, and dear.

A Stack of Shovels

for Jay Wright

> *Silence structures a fragile world; the little day*
> *passes; darkness descends. The expansive touch*
> *of prayer makes love a random walk.*

And throughout the day a genteel silence
gripped us. We saw our mouths as structures
capable of speaking without tongues. Not a
word unsaid, per se, but folded paragraphs fragile
on our lips. Sentences unfolding a little world
we thought we owned—our bodies' entry. The
numbed cruelness we inherited, scoffing little
joys as nuisances. How were we to pass day-
light over to us? Claim a possession? Passes
through paths thought reserved for darkness.
Who was to come for us? Who dare descends
into this ominous arrival and waits patiently? The
aide mèmoire sitting at our sides. Its expansive
pages detailing our grimaces, weighted touch
of our lives: of solitudes, of aspirations, of
all the unsaid etceteras. The closed prayer
hiding in the ellipsis of our sentences makes
and breaks us into some poor form of love,
an undoing we coveted and held onto as a
guide sign to help us navigate life's random
order. No direction, but knowing to walk.

The irresponsible notion of being,
and of that peculiar dispossession
that becomes a form of freedom.

Aren't we like the land beneath after its razing? The
soil's chagrin at our fiery unclothing. An irresponsible

human impulse to set ablaze the nascent, under the notion
there was something to destroy for our creation. What of

my malignant deeds? How have I handled my being—
considering the berry bush vines I have uprooted and

the nesting termites I engulfed in paraffin oil, of
my participation in this tragedy? How uncouth that

I find my aperture in this ontological and peculiar
expense. A supreme truth I've come to love as my dispossession.

This lonesome anguish like a rusty copper wire that
holds no somber bird to rest its talons on. This becomes

the narrative I recite to will my solitary life into motion. A
frigid psalm begging its charged words for warmth. A form-

less prayer I hope claws its etude to higher airs. But of
this I also know, in my divine sacrilege I find freedom.

I will insist upon my body's endurable grammar
even as the world grows silent, or gives in
to a creative forgetfulness.

At dawn's daunting breath, it stretches out its angular ends and I
remain transfixed. In awe that this body is mine to adorn—to will
it into motion. An act reminiscent of a woman I loved who insist-
ed I eat the feta she tried to convince me was paneer, which upon
itself is love's logic. It is staring at the moon, God's lazy eye. My
gaze into that muffled light I anointed holy. Forgetting my own body's
divinity. The summation of it all being our meticulous and endurable
proclivity to find beginnings in endings. Our lives, a forced grammar,
sound as an operational fountain during a rainstorm. Even
I at times cannot contend with living. The ways I hold my days as
a conjunction holds a run-on. Where then to linger in the
fold of it all? A small enclosure or din I will fashion into a world;
I want to protrude as a weed in winter. A minor figure who grows
in tantamount hours. To obtain a purity of sound only silent
as a sequestered second. I do not want to move as an intransigent or
a contrarian; I find faith in believing my being. What it gives
in staying the uncharted course and accepting a human truth, in-
certitude. Here I have furnished an unfinished map where to
reach destination's tail end is to retrace life's preludes. A
sweetness like the carcass of flowers. A misanthropic creative-
ness or idolatry insisting the body's survival is its forgetfulness.

That Same Pain, That Same Pleasure

                    I want to be amorphous.
To linger in my body
and not be held by it.
                    Sometimes what I feel
has a difficult name. I want to hold
something outside
                    my body. Have a serrated
beak for a mouth, but still
carry a gentleness
                    to clasp and not snap
the loose limbs of a tree
then build a lofty nest,
                    but lately I fold into
something amiable with
gawking teeth; a boy
                    who walks staggeredly
to keep his cool. Night
makes a muffled sound
                    and I resound into something
leaking light. Somedays
I ask am I log-bodied?
                    Soaked in smoke to release
my cry at the fires setting
me ablaze—the crackle
                    with which I break.

Frame Ten

after *Chungking Express* (Wong Kar-wai, 1994)

My dreams are becoming more cinematic. Last night I dreamt in black and white
before waking into color like Tarkovsky's *Stalker*. What I mean is I am still not quite
settled in my body. Night's color scheme makes a tie-dyed shadow out of me. I'm all
chiaroscuro. An airy signature on the wind's breath. What marks me is the slight light
showing me shimmer like mist. My escape into sepia. How sunset makes a city look
charred. I think of the woman walking at my side. Light balances a hundred hues on
her frame. Becoming phantom of light and shadow. I want to weave the reflections
into a floating mole at the side of her lips. To sculpt the refracted hues into drapes of
aurora. Become prisoners in a prism of light scrapes, then place a kiss to contort its
glare, leaving my airy signature in a bruised and brayed pair of touches upon her face.

Amrita Sher-Gil Introductory Wall Texts

for Vivan Sundaram

Study for Composition, 1936
75 x 103 cm, Simla

Primarily, I compose from posed subjects. The use of the imagination operates as how to expand upon the rendering of the subject. In *Study for Composition*, the subject, a man, appears "half-finished." He faces the ground while the "finished" side of his body shows a dark and elongated right arm and leg. The fading, tattered white clothes on his back facing the viewer are in contrast, or in correlation, to the shade of brown dust on the opposing side of his body. A thin shawl covers his shoulders, brushing against the gray, once white, turban on his head. The rest of him all drips of paint. The opposing side of his body barely visible. The painting beckons the viewer to ask whether this is in fact a composition or a decomposition? Is the viewer's gaze what renders him animate or inanimate as much as the painter's skill? The point being that good art always tends towards simplification. That is to say, it only considers the essentials of a form. The stress is invariably laid on the textural and structural beauty of the work instead of the subject depicted. Form is never imitated, it is always interpreted. The aim of art being the deprival of aesthetic emotion from abstract beauty, the vitality of line, form, color and design, as opposed to the pleasure derived from the prettiness of the object depicted in the picture. Left to their own initiative, the great majority of people lapse into the common error of trying to discover in pictures emotional pegs on which to hang their feelings and imagine what they derive from the process is synonymous with the real aesthetic emotion the initiated derive from the contemplation of sheer pictorial beauty.

Professional Model, 1933

72 x 100 cm, Paris

The body Valadonian or Albright's Ida. Pale-pink and clay-like limbs elongated across the frame. Grayness of Paris outside the slanted window in the background. Only the muffled room we are privy to and its containment of the squalid composure of a woman sitting naked on an oak chair. Maybe resisting mythic and ersatz female bodies. Her black matted hair with its ends slinking across the powdered, swollen forehead. Eyes like blackened opals. Mouth smeared with the dull nub of a fading red lipstick. Drooping breast split falling to the sides. Her body a system of emotions and triggers lost. Every hair lost in the bath. Every dead cell rubbed off on a towel.

Woman on Charpoy, June 1940
85 x 72.4 cm, Saraya

The scene is all pleasure. Room's faint glow from the lamp at bedside. Tin cup at the side of a clay gourd hoarding fresh water. Mughal table balancing their weight until a dry throat comes to wet the mouth. If thirst is lust, the charpoy is where the body negotiates. A bronze-faced woman with a look of indifference. Body covered in a red sari spotted with black beads. Red alta dye streaks across her scalp, hands, and feet. The assumed position she takes depends on perspective or want. Her budding bosom tugging against the sari. Right hand above her head surrendering to the cloth. Eyes closed while the left snakes close to the pelvis. Left leg spread wide. The right weak in its collapse on the far side of the charpoy. A black sheet embroidered with flower petals drips over the floor where a dark-faced servant sits at the side. She holds a fan fashioned like a small axe—staring at the sprawled body—ready to cool or kill the pleasure.

Self-Portrait as a Tahitian, 1934
56 x 90 cm, Paris

Here I am as a troglodyte, Gauguin's morbid fantasy, a bare body against the frame. Phantom copy of Teha'amana. My hands folded across the pelvis, child-like. A blue cloth separating me from Gauguin. My hair wild country pressed along the spine. Lucid eyes and a clasped mouth marked by a mole hanging at the jaw. The background the play of shadows, each to their savagery. Watercolor splotches of a primordial figure growing within my body. Almost paradisiacal and animal-like. Gauguin, does my body howl? Which of me is more the exotic, the Hungarian or Indian? Which body to commit treason and hide behind the law of savagery?

Red Verandah, May 1938
71.6 x 144.2 cm, Simla

The return began with a vision of winter in India. Endless tracks of luminous yellow-gray land. Dark-bodied and sad-faced men and women over which an indefinable melancholy reigned. They moved silently, almost like silhouettes. The scene of tree trunks colored red in Simla. Open windows of the Holme letting in natural light where I stared outside thinking of plein air paintings. Indira at bedside in incomplete breaths. Barefooted girls outside my window with soft brown earth wedged between their toes. Bodies close enough for their breath to pass warmth. Jittering heads like hives of yellow, orange, and maroon saris consuming them. Tips of their braided ponytails dipped in red alta. Hands clasped in prayer. Angles of their palms like fatigued diamonds as they measured the contours of their faces against the sunset's glow.

Woman at Bath, c. 1940
70 x 92 cm, Saraya

The nude body seated on a black metal stool. Blue brassiere hanging on a nail pressed into the wall where she has water drawn for her bath. At her side, black clay pots filled with warm water, a small plate holding an amber-colored block of soap. Her hair in a bobby pin bun as she looks to her left, ensuring her privacy. She holds a brown clay pot of water ready to douse herself. The water slides along her back, merging with the stretch-mark trails and curling around the exposed right breast. Water continues along her torso. Her body formed into a pitcher. It is the body I know, which is to say it is mine. The weighted eyes in her silence. What is the viewer's gaze, but an invasion? Her slight twist left to keep her front hidden. Her unacknowledgment of the water's current on her back. Her mouth upward; the mist of her breath left as a watermark.

Child Wife, March 1936

53 x 76 cm, Saraya

She sat in a corner of the room. Away from all the women sitting on silk and satin coverlets spread across the floor. Bodies jaundiced in robes of gold, silver, sparkling rubies, and diamonds. Your eyes got sore looking at the dazzling whiteness of the oval or round-shaped pearls which hung in ropes around their necks, sending their glittering rays around the edges of the room where the little bride sat pale and silent. Her lips frothy with red lipstick against the darkness of her face. Hands stained with the redness she wiped from the corners of her mouth. Her hair parted, giving way to a streak of red alta, hints of it in a few strands of her hair. A gold septum ring resting on her upper lip. Eyes wide and dark with a look of indifference. Her only sari patterned with sunflowers and butterflies, covering half her face in the darkness of the corner. Does she think of daughters? Of sons to force through? Of Teha'amana, thirteen too, at bed-side with Gauguin? Her silence breaking into a gruff voice when she responds, *I take him to take me.*

Mother India, June 1935
62 x 78 cm, Simla

They rested fireside as they moved their children closer to its warmth. Hands fanning small logs needing to breathe more flames. Betel leaves and fennel seeds prepared into paan. Weaved baskets they carried and placed sunflowers into as an alibi for their absence. The whistling the flowers made when tossed into fire; their aroma a burning spring or autumn. In their silence, what did they hold in the small passageways they made with their hands fastened to their mouths? I imagine the two children at the side, Indira and I, under the cover of an Indian mother never had. A country we tug against in whom it belongs to—who we belong to. At times my brush slipped and the image became the western projection of India's wilderness I harbored. My promenading in Paris at École des Beaux-Arts when I started wearing saris, believing I was exotic too. Fantasies of savages in wild enclaves. Their dark shades I wanted as mine on canvas.

The Last Unfinished Painting, November 1941
65.7 x 87.5 cm, Lahore

The afterlife is a room with a gashed bulb, pulps of light spitting out into darkness's mouth. A small window opening to a terrace. Outside, trees formed without branches clouded in spongy leaves. Saris clad on bodies drawn as streaks of brown and beige. Opaque yellow and brown buildings. A man working on his roof with clay plates to keep the rain away from his family. A bridge with a glossy red painted viaduct, leading to passageways away from Lahore. The lazy farmer who let his black bulls run loose, birds resting on their horns, pecking at flies and ticks. It is the obscurity of the landscape, its lack of details. My life becoming one still life from Paris—a white colander holding green grapes and pears. Or the plein air paintings of Hungary. The *Merry Cemetery* where the sun streaked decently across graves, covering corpses in natural light.

Woman in Red, 1936
53 x 89 cm, Simla

I dream of red alta dye covering bodies. Women in red saris walking with red and gold bangles shaking against their wrists. Luscious red mouths of Hungarian gypsy girls. Long red-ribbon braids of schoolgirls. Red blossoms dripping on red verandahs. Kathakali dancers covered in red. Red murals of Padmanabhapuram and Pattancheri. Red mouths opening to Ajanta caves. Red shadows across Ellora. Red India. Red all the coffee mugs that bared my lips in Montparnasse cafés in Paris. Red brides, grooms. Öcsi's mouth printed with my red lips. Simla and Lahore covered in Red. Red Saraya. My red children had, but never got. The Ganges covered in red flowers. Red rooms covering me in red. Red sheets absorbing me into their folds.

V

Frame Eleven

At the close of foreday morning, shadowed figures emerged.
Holding myself, wondering what I possess. Small nudgings
alongside my body I'm still tender to. A spring breeze coarse
against the skin. Daylight eases into dusk. Leaves trespass
into alley's folds. Their tossing on gravel splitting stems.
Darkness ascends into tents of shadows. A breath escapes me.
I'm still here holding the length of my arms. Checking the pulse
of my bind. These the hours I long most to be bothered by a
touch. How do I reach a home aside from the imagination?
An image insists. I starve for air in some margin of its light.
Streets littered in a burgundy blaze. Wind's breath brushing
leaves off laurels. A small girl watches them fall. Her hands
clutched around dandelions. Her breath without muscle blows
the seeds off. The white fuzz clinging to her shirt before she
lets a quiet sneeze. Her wish is to sleep in a pile of leaves this
spring. Collect lightning bugs in a Mason jar. Make earrings
out of their light then run in the dark like a fading flashlight.
I wish to wrap myself in new flesh, become choranxyptic,
and not fear my body's unpredictability.

Pastoral

In the backfields of my grandparents' farm
in Chikumbi, I fashioned a slingshot

    from a broken branch, formed into
the letter *Y*. Two bands of black and red elastic

    tethered to a pouch nesting a marble. I saw
a lilac-breasted roller, watching me

    from the top of a zebrawood tree. The roller
fluttering its wings to taunt me. I pulled on

the pouch, launching the marble. The body tumbled
    against tree branches before it landed on the soil

    beneath me. The bird on its back, struggling
to flap its dead wing. I forced the marble

    into its delicate mouth, cracking its beak
until the marble protruded in its throat. I laid

    on my back next to the roller. Gently rubbing
the marble. The feathers on the dead wing

    ruffled. I dug a hole and tucked the roller in,
sticking my slingshot in the dirt as a headstone.

    My palms tightly pressed against the grave
to mute the shaking underneath me.

Paean to Chikumbi

for Nguwa Phiri

And the village was steeped
    in red clay soil. Stars whistling
        across sky. Drywood

    termites flying
over us every spring.
        We thought we

    could pluck some if we extended
our little arms, barely
        hopping off the ground.

    Cousins' small greased
        hands sliding down
            grandma's legs, swollen

        with arthritis.
Attempting to force
    the pain into light

tremors. Aunts in
        bold chitenges—
infants strapped to their

        backs, pounding
corn bende na munsi.
        White corn powder

later turned to nshima.
Songs falling from
                    their mouths. My ears

    to the ground, picking up
Bemba lyrics:

        Ubunga bwa male lito
    bwasalangana lito tabumona
                beni lito ale kanshinguluke

ale kanshinguluke kanshinguluke
    ka lito ale kambweluluke
        ale kambweluluke

kambweluluke ka lito.

    My nose to the sky, inhaling
        today's hand-washed
laundry hanging on copper

                wires between mango
    trees. Frothy soap tablets
                in buckets of water

        serving as detergent.
                Scent of mustard greens,
    kandolo, impwa. Papaya tree

        that blossomed one fruit.
We chopped it down.
    So sweet, we ate the seeds.

Fertilizer we placed in
        cornfields. Our skin developing
   rashes for the harvest.

                  Once they bloomed,
            we husked corn silk
                and placed them on

our heads, pretending to be
        bazungu. Sugar cane stalk
we snapped and peeled

            with our teeth. Sometimes
busting our lips. Tasting blood
      in the sweet

                 mulch. Maybe dreaming
            of sugar water and a taste
                    of chitumbuas.

Sand hills where honey
bees formed hives.
   Our hands reaching

        for combs, numbed to the
stinging pain in the name
      of sweetness.

                Tongues licking fresh
           honey off each comb piece
before we passed it

to the next. Blind snakes
grandpa caught
by hand. Severing

heads before wrapping
their bodies in banana leaves
and burning them.

Small sacrifice
or ritual to keep us
alive. Listening

to his omens that forbade
us from pointing at graves.
When my voice

became too rough to him,
the walk he made me take
to the mulberry tree.
Branch
he ordered I snap off myself.
Its body covered

in ripe berries. His swing
of the luscious blows
against my back,

staining my good
shirt tie-dyed with
berry juice. Crowngrass

where we preyed
on grasshoppers before
we roasted them on

woodfire.
           Guava trees I climbed
to glance at chameleons

        nesting. Their changing colors—
chartreuse, tuscany, emerald,
      and lime—

          signaling ripeness.
                  Sometimes malice:
the seasonal floods.

        Soiled streams running
with kapentas.
           We caught kapentas

                  in streams by hand.
        Our oversized shirts
           serving as nets.

     We squatted and cast
       our shirts in the muddy
streams to taste some

           form of nyama. Seasoned
        them with the onions
from grandma's wild garden.

Saving some to rub on our
     bodies, waiting for hair
       to bloom.

            Ancient myths
         we believed. Shock that sent
     me back to the burning

woodstove. My fall in
       the tin tub
filled with boiling water.

      Sores and blisters
          peeling skin off.
            Water's

heat peeled a map
      from my back like
the kapenta's skeleton.

At David Livingstone's Statue

for Harry Mphanza

> We have changed a great many of our colonial place names since independence,
> but we have kept the name of Livingstone out of a deep respect.
> —Siloka Mukuni, chief of the Leya people

At the onset of my ingenious plan, the sun barely shone
     through the mist.
  I struggled with a name to identify the rushes
    of water pouring beside me.

Half of my tongue saying Mosi-oa-Tunya—
"the smoke that thunders." The other saying Victoria Falls.

  And here is my complex. To shred the palettes
     of English lodged on my tongue. Its sheer civility.
     Restraining all languages,

      I snuck past two olive-sheened
security guards sleeping underneath the shade
    of banana leaves to find Livingstone's bronze body

to which I snickered: "Dr. Livingstone, I presume?"
  My hand ran across the chiseled letters inscribed
    across his body. What I read gathered all that was
lost in me, including the anger and sadness I learned as birthright:

[I COME NEITHER AS SAINT NOR SINNER. I AM PREPARED TO GO ANYWHERE,
    PROVIDED IT BE FORWARD]

And maybe more than this was the lush grin I imagined
so carefully plastered on his face, taunting history
                    beyond the grave. The recordings of his barren

solitude heated by poisonous winds, his treks through
the wild jungles infested by snakes and only roamed
        over by a few scattered tribes of untameable barbarians.

I thought of my father's unmarked grave.
            My weekly visits to graveyards in Lusaka,
imagining his body belonging to each bed covered with grass.
                        Small, cracked rocks gathered by children

    to form an altar. My slow words grafting epithets against
airy headstones. I laid on graves imagining my father's funeral
                    and a decent headstone to give my name an origin:

                    I bet he was buried in a bed of blues.
        There must have been wailers;
    the pangs of mothers. Women in droves moaning,
    singing low songs, repenting the grave
        and its folding soils.

            Chitenges were worn, screams buried
        in slow groans, incantations moaned.
    Grave-dancers surrounding the casket,

                limbs moaning
    lost songs, folktales, and fables. The sun brushing
        light on their rags—time they held.
            My father's hand I wished

    I could have held, rusted pasts and dreams
            shaking in his palms.

It's the same sadness I carry when I think of Lumumba's
    exhumed and dissolved body. Pauline left to mourn
                            the imagination of him—

        locating a compass of wounds. Our absence as fitting
                effigies for caskets. It was then I reached
    into the duffle bag where I'd been hoarding
        the Mason jars of piss to shatter against

Livingstone's bronze-cast face.
    The small hammer I brandished to crack the bronze
until I heard a wailing inside. (History's vowels maybe).
    And I was left to my own undoing where I thought

                of the savagery of monuments.
                        The emptiness of bearing one's flag.
        Our profound yet hollow deaths in graves
                where we can't locate our names.

Frame Twelve

Everything has form:
dusk with its desperate colors of erasure;
the hollow, unearthly hour of night;
the lullaby of shadows
unleashing arduous, scintillating silences.
The flavors of tongues—
apertures.
I've imagined it all
and the stretched out ends our lives make.
I am an addict of the human comedy—
the very dirge—
the luster of something.
This is my other heritage.
To forget the impossible weight of being human;
to settle into the flesh of our futures.

Dear Suzanne

I hope you do not mind me writing to you in this manner, but after reading your essay "The Great Camouflage" in the last issue of *Tropiques*, suspended due to the influence of the Vichy Regime in France's colonies, I have arrived at an unequivocal truth, guided by the extraterrestrial musings of Sun Ra about the possibilities of our jaundiced bodies in other worlds. The truth I have arrived at comes from the last cut off Ra's 1978 album with the Arkestra, *Lanquidity*: "There Are Other Worlds (They Have Not Told You Of)." Suzanne, I do apologize if this appears as a fanatical approach, but it was the only way I could stop indulging in solipsisms in order to reach you at the plain you have so vastly, but also meticulously, set.

I cannot think of a greater time for the natal occasion of your essay than this epoch, which is essentially reminiscent of René Ménil's earlier concerns in his 1978 introduction to *Légitime Défense*. Ménil argued for *a cruel aggressive pleasure, a settling of accounts with colonial ugliness (sadism) and also a pleasure of experiencing the wounds received in order to be better able to proclaim the legitimacy of the cause (masochism)*. Which is the same anxiety I believe you and I feel of being human, at least in this present reality where we feel as if we are merely shadows (signatures) of being human. Ultimately, what you and I are called to, our nodal points, as we continue to construct our personal mythologies through writing, is that which Aimé coined as the sur-rational nature of reality. I am no Antillean, but I am also of a captured home. What I have gathered of my histories, laboriously spread out in these pages, is an aspiration to subvert, what I can through writing, the present reality with one grounded in one of those other worlds I hear Ra echoing. Which is why I am a firm believer that what we do, as writers, is a transcendental experience. I am in complete agreement when you write *it [is] imperatively the time for dissent, and essentially for dissident thinking*. This is, after all, our alembics of suffering as it is our ancestral anxiety.

It is here I see Blackness and the longing of our imagination as Janus headed. We must find another nature we can see in the interplay of looking behind and beyond. It is, as you say, Suzanne, in your essay where you conjure the image of the hummingbird and its song. We must cultivate our own song to sing us into an ascent of dissension. Aren't we all just *les sans-papiers* of the world spending time in this reality as the unfathomable layover hours of our lives?

Again, I apologize in advance if my concerns are merely projections, but I do believe what we both seek is *to grasp beyond the known limits of civilizations* with the imagination. To encompass all parts of our Blackness, our métissage, which is really my love for poetry. It is the only genre of art that allows such an expansive, intertextual, transcendental, transnational, and transdisciplinary style in its approach. Poetry is, or should be, about breaching and reaching the possibility of language and its interwoven anguishes. In how we receive language not only from texts but other arts as well in addition to its forceful imprint upon others. Think of all that has been expropriated and appropriated from us, Suzanne. Am I mistaken then to say the imagination is the sole possession we have left? This was my greatest ambition with these poems I have set beside this letter, to exhaust the possibilities of where and how far poetry can go in what I feel is its inherent ekphrastic nature. *It alone conceives of worlds in which man, if he lived in them, would cease to feel himself a stranger.* The possibilities of representation, the Gestalt of the image, and its wholeness severed into text. My intentionality is not the specific as much as it is the peculiarities or frailties of representation. I am called to failure, Suzanne. Regardless, I want to be ever reaching. Infinitely curious. To touch all parts of my being with precision. *To be present in history down to the marrow.* I want to live in the decadent image because I know I revel in understanding its différement. It is how I know I am a dissident being. It is why I turn to poetry for its ability *to transport us into an extraordinary world: the land of the marvellous.* And so, Suzanne, I see all parts of my being as a craft ready to be wielded and willed.

fin

The cento poems "Frame One," "Frame Two," "Frame Three," "Frame Four," "Frame Five," "Frame Six," "Frame Seven," "Frame Eight," "Frame Nine," and "Frame Twelve" along with the non-cento poems "Frame Ten" and "Frame Eleven," are in conversation with Ralph Ellison's Rinehart character in *Invisible Man* and Abbas Kiarostami's final and posthumous film *24 Frames*. Respectfully, the centos are composed entirely of lines from poets, writers, musicians, and filmmakers. I want to emphasize that these centos are not traditional. Rather, they are experimental. Regarding a few of the lines used for the centos, minor mechanical changes were made for punctuation and grammatical purposes. In the notes below, I have provided the author, musician, filmmaker, or poet; the name of the passage section, poem, or song the line was taken from; the book or album in which the poem, passage section, or song was written in; and I provide the lines used in my centos as they connect to the aforementioned sources. Worth noting that some of the lines I used were found in texts that did not contain passage sections, titles, or any other specific identifying factors. For those lines, I attributed the author's name and the name of the source in which I drew that particular line from. In addition, some of these lines are drawn from the same poems or passage sections. Lastly, for some of the lines, I have used lines from various text sources written by the same author (i.e., Agha Shahid Ali, Lynda Hull, Nathaniel Mackey, Michael Ondaatje, etc.). See notes below:

Frame One uses lines from:

Agha Shahid Ali, "By Exiles," *Call Me Ishmael Tonight: A Book of Ghazals*
   "Autumn's mist pressed to ashes"

Carl Phillips, "A Great Noise," *Quiver of Arrows: Selected Poems, 1986–2006*
  "The musculature"

Claude McKay, "The Tropics in New York," *Selected Poems*
  "My eyes grew dim and I could no more gaze"

David Ferry translation, "Tablet One," *Gilgamesh*
  "The perfect, the terror"

Gwendolyn Brooks, "Chapter Two—Spring Landscape: Detail," *Maud Martha*
  "The sky was gray, but the sun was making little silver promises"

Li-Young Lee, "The Gift," *Rose*
  "Voice still, a well of dark water, a prayer"

Lynda Hull, "Fairy Tales: Steel Engravings," *Star Ledger*
  "Thin collars of fog"

Lynda Hull, "The Fitting," *The Collected Poems*, edited by David Wojahn
  "My tongue was difficult"

Lynda Hull, "Star Ledger," *Star Ledger*
  "Names meant to conjure sultry nights"

Michael Ondaatje, *The Collected Works of Billy the Kid*
  "A public breathing through the night"

Michael Ondaatje, Section One: Asian Rumours, "Asia," *Running in the Family*
  "What began it all was the bright bone of a dream I could hardly hold."

Michael Ondaatje, Section One: There's a Trick with a Knife I'm Learning to Do,
  "Signature," *The Cinnamon Peeler*
  "I stretched all senses"
  "I bended in particular angles"

Ralph Ellison, Chapter Sixteen, *Invisible Man*
  "I was somehow attuned to it all"

Ralph Ellison, Chapter Twenty-Two, *Invisible Man*
  "Forgotten names sang through my head"
  "And I began to tremble so violently"

Stanley Kunitz, "End of Summer" in *The Collected Poems*
  "A perturbation of the light;"

Terrance Hayes, "How to Draw an Invisible Man," *How to Be Drawn*
  "And because I mean to live transparently, I am here, bear with me, describing the contents."

Tim Seibles, "Blade Unplugged," *Fast Animal*
  "That breaks what's left of what's human in me"

Tim Seibles, "Later," *Fast Animal*
  "I don't know what I'm becoming"

Tim Seibles, "Vendetta, May 2006," *Fast Animal*
  "The wind tilting slowly;"

Vladimir Nabokov, Section Two, Chapter Two, *Speak Memory*
  "I lingered a little to listen to the singing in my ears"

The Code of Hammurabi uses the line "even their shadows hostile," which is taken from Édouard Glissant's poem "Lavas" in the collection *Riveted Blood* from *The Collected Poems of Édouard Glissant*, translated by Jeff Humphries.

Frame Two uses lines from:

Antonio Machado, "Tranquil Afternoon, Almost," *Border of a Dream: Selected Poems*, translated by Willis Barnstone
  "To have had some joys and to tenderly recall them"

Ariana Reines, "Rite Aid," *Mercury*
  "How aspects of myself could be rendered"

Carl Phillips, "Death of the Sibyl," *Quiver of Arrows: Selected Poems 1986–2006*
  "The rush of whole lives passing elsewhere without you"

Dawn Lundy Martin, *Discipline*
  "Being adrift in place"

Lynda Hull, "Ornithology," *The Collected Poems*, edited by David Wojahn
  "A way of breaking synchronistic through time"

Merrill Moore, "No Comment," *XxX: 100 Poems*, edited by David R. Slavitt
"How tragic the force of destiny can be"

Nathaniel Mackey, "Kiche Manitou," *Eroding Witness*
"I awoke ahead of myself"

Nathaniel Mackey, "Song of the Andoumboulou: 8," *School of Udhra*
"Night like so many such nights I've known"

Rainer Maria Rilke, "The First Elegy," *Duino Elegies and the Sonnets to Orpheus*, translated by Stephen Mitchell
"Strange to see meanings that clung together once"

Rainer Maria Rilke, "The Tenth Elegy," *Duino Elegies and the Sonnets to Orpheus*, translated by Stephen Mitchell
"How we squander our hours of pain"

Sohrab Sepehri, "Sunlight," *The Oasis of Now: Selected Poems*, translated by Kazim Ali and Mohammad Jafar Mahallati
"Snow's echo, time raining down"

Stanley Kunitz, "I Dreamed That I Was Old," *The Collected Poems*
"I wept with bitter longing, not remembering how in my youth I cried"

Vladimir Nabokov, Part One: Section Eleven, *Lolita*
"Warm dusk had deepened into amorous darkness"

Wallace Stevens, "Hibiscus on the Sleeping Shores," *The Collected Poems: The Corrected Edition*
"The mind roamed as a moth roams"

Frame Three uses lines from:

Abdellatif Laâbi, "Chronicle of the Citadel of Exile," *In Praise of Defeat*, translated by Donald Nicholson-Smith
"I listen and little by little I perceive that voice's harmony"

Agha Shahid Ali, "From Another Desert," *A Nostalgist's Map of America*
"Everywhere the shadows of my voice"

Afaa Michael Weaver, "The Kidnappers," *A Hard Summation*
"A cruel silence in the night"

Bob Kaufman, "Picasso's Balcony," *The Ancient Rain: Poems, 1956–1978*
"Pale morning light dying in shadows"
"Blue flames burning"

Brigit Pegeen Kelly, "The Column of Mercury Recording the Temperature of Night," *Song*
"It makes a flute-like sound"
"A sound like held breath escaping"

Cathy Park Hong, "Rite of Passage," *Translating Mo'um*
"The arterial clouds shouldered a glassy reservoir"

Christopher Gilbert, "Kite-Flying," *Across the Mutual Landscape*
"Their lives the way stars hold to the sky"

Lynda Hull, "So Many Swimmers," *Star Ledger*
"Confettied to shreds, the last leaves darken gusts"

Natasha Trethewey, "Genus Narcissus," *Native Guard*
"I must have seen in them some measure of myself"

Tim Seibles, "Later," *Fast Animal*
"The birds repeat a warning I think I should understand"

T. S. Eliot, "Portrait of a Lady," *The Collected Poems, 1909–1962*
"Absurdly hammering a prelude of its own"
"Capricious monotone"

Frame Four uses lines from:

A. Van Jordan, "After 75 Years Greenwood, Oklahoma, Gets a Statue," *Rise*
"One child runs past, stops, and bends to secure his loose shoelace"

A. Van Jordan, "Red Ball Express," *Macnolia*
"A silence grows too loud to ignore"

Agha Shahid Ali, "For You," *Call Me Ishmael Tonight: A Book of Ghazals*
  "Something like smoke rises from the snuffed-out distance"

Agha Shahid Ali, "I Dream I Am the Only Passenger On Flight 423 to Srinagar,"
  The Country without a Post Office
  "Before ash filigrees roses carved in the wood of weeping trees"

Amiri Baraka, "Numbers, Letters," *SOS: Poems, 1961–2013*
  "A long breath singer"

Anne Carson, "Geryon," *Autobiography of Red*
  "Hobbles in the red wind"

Antonio Machado, "The Voyager," *Border of a Dream: Selected Poems*, translated by
  Willis Barnstone
  "In the old melancholy park, leaves spin out of autumn"

Ben Lerner, *The Lichtenberg Figures*
  "Shadows cast shadows ad infinitum"

Bob Kaufman, "Arrival," *The Ancient Rain: Poems, 1956–1978*
  "The crawling day arrives on skinned knees"
  "Old men fighting death in secret corners"

Bob Kaufman, "Picasso's Balcony," *The Ancient Rain: Poems, 1956–1978*
  "Dancing blue images, shades of blue pasts"

Bob Kaufman, "Scene in a Third Eye," *The Ancient Rain: Poems, 1956–1978*
  "Pinned into air, stuck in time"

Brigit Pegeen Kelly, "Field Song," *Song*
  "A fawn figure with a filigreed grin"

Christopher Gilbert, "Metaphor for Something That Plays Us: Remembering Eric
  Dolphy," *Turning into Dwelling*
  "I walk closer to the traffic's noise"

Christopher Okigbo, "Fragments Out of the Deluge," *Labyrinths and Path of
  Thunder*
  "A small bird sings in shadows"

Claude McKay, "Song in New Hampshire," *Selected Poems*
  "Too green the springing April grass"

Common, "The Corner," *Be*
  "Look to the sky, hope it bleeds light"

Donika Kelly, "Love Poem: Minotaur," *Bestiary*
  "A golden light hails me"

Esther Phillips, "Legacy," *The Stone Gatherer*
  "Everything was fortissimo"

Harryette Mullen, *Notes from A Tanka Diary: Urban Tumbleweed*
  "Leave fingers brushed with yellow pollen"

Jay Wright, "Some Say the Spirit Does No Work. All Greek," *Disorientations: Groundings*
  "Silence that structures a voice in the dark"

Li-Young Lee, "The City in Which I Love You," *The City In Which I Love You*
  "I mount the scabbed streets, the long shouts of avenues"

Li-Young Lee, "For a New Citizen of the United States," *The City In Which I Love You*
  "And in the interval between familiar faces, events occurred"

Li-Young Lee, "Furious Versions," *The City In Which I Love You*
  "Someone whispering into someone's ear, someone crying behind a door"

Li-Young Lee, "The Gift," *Rose*
  "A silver tear, a tiny flame"

Li-Young Lee, "Persimmons," *Rose*
  "Warm as my face"

Lynda Hull, "Love Song during Riot with Many Voices," *Star Ledger*
  "Traffic stalls to bricks shattering"
  "Storefront churches asking for mercy"

Lynda Hull, "Utopia Parkway," *Star Ledger*
  "And the whole bedazzled city's a magnificent arcade."

Mary Oliver, "Mushrooms," *American Primitive*
"Astonishing in their suddenness, their quietude, their wetness"

Nathaniel Mackey, "Song of the Andoumboulou: 5," *Eroding Witness*
"The slight rub of untongued voices"

Ralph Ellison, Chapter Five, *Invisible Man*
"The sudden arpeggios of laughter lilting across"
"Voices soft in the mellow dusk"
"The decorous walking around me, sounds of footsteps"

Ralph Ellison, Chapter Twenty-Three, *Invisible Man*
"A mysterious blur to a soft sinister glowing"

Rigoberto González, "Before the First Man Stepped On the Moon," *So Often the Pitcher Goes to Water until It Breaks*
"To tempt our hands"

Sohrab Sepehri, "The Living Word," *The Oasis of Now: Selected Poems*, translated by Kazim Ali and Mohammad Jafar Mahallati
"Someone grieves or weaves, counts or sings"

Sohrab Sepehri, "Sunlight," *The Oasis of Now: Selected Poems*, translated by Kazim Ali and Mohammad Jafar Mahallati
"Sounds of water pouring"
"Damp, wet bricks and stones, clean bones of daylight"

Sohrab Sepehri, "Water's Footfall," *The Oasis of Now: Selected Poems*, translated by Kazim Ali and Mohammad Jafar Mahallati
"I saw the sprouts and plants growing through light and then darkness"
"Light coughs in the bushes"
"Chirping swallows slip, dripping down through the roof of spring"
"The train sped by with its cargo of light"
"I saw a street sweeper praying, pressing his forehead on a melon rind"
"The driver longing for death"
"A crack in the wall fights the persistent advances of the sunlight"
"The rain-wet alleys"
"Humans in darkness and in light"

Terrance Hayes, "At Pegasus," *Muscular Music*
"And I am not that far away"

Terrance Hayes, "Yummy Suite: Blues," *Muscular Music*
"Sun out like a floodlight"

Theodore Roethke, "The Coming of the Cold," *The Collected Poems*
"The ribs of leaves lie in the dust"

Theodore Roethke, "Flower Dump," *The Collected Poems*
"Whole beds of bloom pitched on a pile"

Tim Seibles, "4 A.M.," *Fast Animal*
"Sky like the inside of a skillet and bright as ghosts"

Lester Leaps In is after the jazz single of the same name, dedicated to tenor saxophonist Lester Young, by Count Basie's Kansas City Seven.

Frame Five uses lines from:

Afaa Michael Weaver, "Spirit Boxing," *Spirit Boxing*
"My body a heavy meat on bones"

Ariana Reines, "Book Forgive Everything," *The Cow*
"A sleeve of light"
"A radiance inside of time"

Ariana Reines, Section Two: Save the World, *Mercury*
"I must be responsible for it"

Ariana Reines, "Se Trouver Dans Un Trou, Au Fond D'un Trou," *The Cow*
"An assurance"

César Vallejo, "Poem to Be Read and Sung," *The Complete Poetry*, translated by Clayton Eshleman
"I know there is a person composed of my parts"

Edward Hirsch, "What the Goddess Can Do," *The Living Fire: New and Selected Poems*
"I have been many things in this life"

Gerald Barrax, "I Travel with Her," *From A Person Sitting In Darkness: New and Selected Poems*
"Too often not having proof of myself"

June Jordan, "Let Me Live with Marriage," *Directed by Desire: The Collected Poems*
"I am black within as is this skin"

Frame Six uses lines from:

Antonio Machado, "I Have Walked Many Roads," *Border of a Dream: Selected Poems*, translated by Willis Barnstone
"In every place I've watched caravans of sorrow"

A. Van Jordan, "Looking for Work," *Macnolia*
"I run like all the other men, chasing my shadow down alleys"

Bhanu Kapil, "What is the Shape of Your Body?" *The Vertical Interrogation of Strangers*
"Sometimes in the spaces, there is fear"

Dawn Lundy Martin, *Discipline*
"Not so much a name, but the result of a name"
"It's a strange sensation to yell out: this is me!"

Inger Christensen, "Letter in April," *Light, Grass, and Letter in April*, translated by Susanna Nied
"Who knows, maybe I myself am called something other than myself"

Li-Young Lee, "Furious Versions," *The City In Which I Love You*
"These days I wake in the used light of someone's spent life"

Patrick Rosal, "Despedida between Cities," *Boneshepherds*
"I keep remembering everything in two time zones at once"

Patrick Rosal, "Throwing Down a Book of Poems I Run toward an Open Window Then Down into the Street to Chase Strange Music," *Boneshepherds*
"The voice rises on a storm of grackles, then returns—half elegy, half serenade"

Rainer Maria Rilke, "The Book of a Monastic Life," *The Book of Hours: Love Poems to God*, translated by Anita Barrows and Joanna Macy
"My mind deepens into them"

Robert Hayden, "From the Corpse Woodpiles, from the Ashes," *The Collected Poems*
"In light part nightmare and part vision fleeing"

Sohrab Sepehri, "Water's Footfall," *The Oasis of Now: Selected Poems*, translated by Kazim Ali and Mohammad Jafar Mahallati
"I have no place of origin, no home"

Terrance Hayes, "What Was the Role of Chance?" *To Float in the Space Between*
"I am often a stranger to myself"

Tim Seibles, "Later," *Fast Animal*
"From calm to fear my mind moves, then moves"

Open Casket Body Double for Patrice Lumumba's Funeral uses the lines "I write you these words not knowing whether you will receive them, when you will receive them, and whether I will still be alive when you read them"; "Its right to an honorable life, to perfect dignity, to independence with no restrictions"; and "Do not weep for me, my companion. History will have its day one day" from Patrice Lumumba's "Letter from Thysville Prison to Mrs. Lumumba" in *May Our People Triumph: Poem, Speeches, and Interviews* by Patrice Lumumba, edited by Sankar Srinivasan.

Notes toward a Biography of Henry Tayali uses the lines in the section labeled *A Measure of Cooking Oil*. Woodcut "I remain a son of my country. I am a fragment of it. A particle" from Andrei Tarkovsky's *Sculpting in Time*, chapter 6: "The Author in Search of an Audience." In addition to that same section, the lines "My art is concerned with the suffering of the people. I want it to be the echo of that suffering. I see the problems of the continent. I am recording what I and my people feel, but I do not attempt to provide answers" are from the article "Rapacious Birds and Severed Heads: Early Bronze Rings from Nigeria," which appears in *African Arts* 13, no. 3 (May, 1980): 82–84. Lastly, the section labeled *Pounding Maize. Woodcut* uses the lines "thought is brief, whereas the image is absolute" from Andrei Tarkovksy's *Sculpting in Time*, chapter 2: "Art—A Yearning for the Ideal."

Frame Seven uses lines from:

Abdellatif Laâbi, "Death of Mine," *In Praise of Defeat*, translated by Donald
  Nicholson-Smith
  "I want you as a tremor of dawn"

Brenda Shaughnessy, "Spring in Space: A Lecture," *Human Dark with Sugar*
  "Your hands find me where there is no science, only precision"

Christopher Gilbert, "Glimpses," *Across the Mutual Landscape*
  "Breath hanging overhead, a fever to the sky"

Christopher Gilbert, "Horizontal Cosmology," *Across the Mutual Landscape*
  "You take my breath"
  "You this world's blue thirst"

Esther Phillips, "And Yet Again," *Leaving Atlantis*
  "Your way past your old hurts, crumbling like dust"

Esther Phillips, "Arrival," *Leaving Atlantis*
  "Your vows of homecoming"

Esther Phillips, "Nexus," *The Stone Gatherer*
  "You swear sometimes I am your nemesis, even"
  "I am your dotage, your vulnerable season"

Esther Phillips, "Night Errant," *Leaving Atlantis*
  "You deny, you deny, you deny"

Esther Phillips, "Paper-Trailing," *Leaving Atlantis*
  "Your sorting, tearing, putting aside"

Esther Phillips, "Runner," *The Stone Gatherer*
  "You who pluck consonants like silver from the generous air"

Esther Phillips, "Unseen," *Leaving Atlantis*
  "Your deep-throated discourse"

Esther Phillips, "Unwritten Poem," *The Stone Gatherer*
  "Your sleeping form"
  "Your secret passions into being"

Esther Phillips, "You Another Country," *Leaving Atlantis*
  "You are yourself another country"

Harryette Mullen, *Notes from A Tanka Diary: Urban Tumbleweed*
  "Your kindling limbs, branches of extinguished blossoms"

June Jordan, "Poem for Nana," *Directed by Desire: The Collected Poems*
  "I find my way by following your spine"

Luljeta Lleshanaku, "Chamomile Breath," *Fresco*, edited by Henry Israeli
  "Your chamomile breath"

Luljeta Lleshanaku, "Electrolytes," *Fresco*, edited by Henry Israeli
  "And your breath disappearing in my lungs"

Nathaniel Mackey, "Ghede Poem," *Eroding Witness*
  "Your own belated breath"

Nathaniel Mackey, "Ghost of a Chance," *Eroding Witness*
  "Your mouth recites a wordless vow"

Nathaniel Mackey, "Solomon's Outer Wall," *Eroding Witness*
  "Our day, serenaded by dust"

Nathaniel Mackey, "Song of the Andoumboulou: 3," *Eroding Witness*
  "Mouth that moved my mouth to song"

Sohrab Sepehri, "Sunlight," *The Oasis of Now: Selected Poems*, translated by Kazim Ali and Mohammad Jafar Mahallati
  "Some voyagers dream of you walking through their twisting lanes"

Sohrab Sepehri, "When Night Flooded Over," *The Oasis of Now: Selected Poems*, translated by Kazim Ali and Mohammad Jafar Mahallati
  "The pressure of your exhale"
  "Your slight shifting"

Frame Eight uses lines from:

Abbas Kiarostami, "A Wolf on Watch," *In The Shadow of Trees: The Collected Poetry*,
   translated by Iman Tavassoly and Paul Cronin
   "I am free of limitations"

Abdellatif Laâbi, "Chronicle of the Citadel of Exile," *In Praise of Defeat*, translated
   by Donald Nicholson-Smith
   "Tonight and all the nights to come"
   "The future contains nothing uncertain"

Abdellatif Laâbi, "I Dare to Speak of My Darkness," *In Praise of Defeat*, translated
   by Donald Nicholson-Smith
   "I dare to speak of my darkness"

Abdellatif Laâbi, "Talisman's Eye," *In Praise of Defeat*, translated by Donald
   Nicholson-Smith
   "I know what power inhabits me"

Abdellatif Laâbi, "Sensation," *In Praise of Defeat*, translated by Donald
   Nicholson-Smith
   "I am here eyes half-open clinging to the thread that sews day to night"

Amiri Baraka, "Gatsby's Theory of Aesthetics," *SOS: Poems, 1961–2013*
   "But also to invest the world with a clearer understanding of itself"

Amiri Baraka, "Numbers, Letters," *SOS: Poems, 1961–2013*
   "I will say nothing that I feel is a lie or unproven"

André Breton, "The Verb to Be," *Earthlight: Poems*, translated by Bill Zavatsky and
   Zack Rogow
   "I know the general outline of despair"

Anne Sexton, "Suicide Note," *The Complete Poems*
   "I will be a light thing"

Anne Sexton, "The Truth the Dead Know," *The Complete Poems*
   "I cultivated myself where the sun gutters from the sky"

Clarice Lispector, *Água Viva*
"Everything has an instant in which it is"

Claudia Rankine, "Testimonial," *The End of the Alphabet*
"The hurt this world could give"

Dawn Lundy Martin, *Discipline*
"Every silent wailing could find its place in these acts"
"Fragments of being; being or nothing; near not being"

Federico García Lorca, "Rooster," *Collected Poems*
"I want clear days and nights and no secrets"

June Jordan, "Who Look at Me, Who See," *Directed by Desire: The Collected Poems*
"Although the world forgets me"

Luljeta Lleshanaku, "Self-Portrait in Silica," *Child of Nature*, translated by Henry Israeli & Shpresa Qatipi
"I will have a voice, a color"

Merrill Moore, "In Re: Sonnets That Choose to Arrive at Meal Time," *XxX: 100 Poems*, edited by David R. Slavitt
"The web of the inner levels of the mind"

Theodore Roethke, "Open House," *The Collected Poems*
"My truths are all foreknown"

Tim Seibles, "Momentum," *Hurdy-Gurdy*
"This slight tickling, this light madness"

T. S. Eliot, "The Love Song of J. Alfred Prufrock," *Collected Poems, 1909–1962*
"For I have known them all already, known them all"

T. S. Eliot, "One," *Collected Poems, 1909–1962*
"I rejoice that things are as they are"

T. S. Eliot, "Silence," *Collected Poems, 1909–1962*
"The wheels of circumstance that grind so terribly within the mind"

Wallace Stevens, "The Plot against the Giant," *The Collected Poems: The Corrected Edition*
   "I shall whisper heavenly labials in a world of gutturals"

Auteur Poetica uses the lines "Each writer finds a new entrance into the mystery" from the preface of Lu Chi's *Wen Fu: The Art of Writing*, translated by Sam Hamill.

Frame Nine uses lines from:

Abdellatif Laâbi, from "Address from the Arab Hill" (1985), *In Praise of Defeat*, translated by Donald Nicholson-Smith
   "I invite you to a moment of truth"

Abdellatif Laâbi, "In Praise of Defeat," *In Praise of Defeat*, translated by Donald Nicholson-Smith
   "I would like to believe in the reality of my body and its needs"

Amiri Baraka, "The Liar," *SOS: Poems, 1961–2013*
   "Even its comforts are hideous uses I strain to understand"

Amiri Baraka, "The New Sheriff," *SOS: Poems, 1961–2013*
   "There is something in me so cruel, so silent"

Amiri Baraka, "Numbers, Letters," *SOS: Poems, 1961–2013*
   "I can't say who I am unless you agree I'm real"

Brigit Pegeen Kelly, "Divining the Field," *Song*
   "It is too much to bear sometimes"

Dawn Lundy Martin, *Discipline*
   "I, too, am often misrecognized in the dark"

Mary Oliver, "August," *American Primitive*
   "All day my body accepts what it is"

Merrill Moore, "Cutie," *XxX: 100 Poems*, edited by David R. Slavitt
   "Something dark, lustful, dangerous, and dear"

T. S. Eliot, "Gerontion," *Collected Poems, 1909–1962*
   "A dull head among windy spaces"

A Stack of Shovels is a series of golden shovels using the lines "Silence structures a fragile world; the little day passes; darkness descends. The expansive touch of prayer makes love a random walk" from *Music's Mask and Measure*; the lines "The irresponsible notion of being, and of that peculiar dispossession that becomes a form of freedom" are from *Disorientations: Groundings*; and the lines "I will insist upon my body's endurable grammar even as the world grows silent, or gives in to a creative forgetfulness" are from *Polynomials and Pollen: Parables, Proverbs, Paradigms, and Praise for Lois*. All these works belong to Jay Wright.

That Same Pain, That Same Pleasure is after Ralph Ellison's interview with Richard G. Stern from his collection *Shadow and Act* and uses the line "Sometimes what I feel has a difficult name" from Terrance Hayes's poem "God Is an American" from *Lighthead*.

Amrita Sher-Gil Introductory Wall Texts uses the lines "The return began with a vision of winter in India. Endless tracks of luminous yellow-gray land. Dark bodied and sad-faced men and women over which an indefinable melancholy reigned" in the *Red Verandah*, May 1938 section from Vivan Sundaram's *Amrita Sher-Gil: A Self-Portrait in Letters and Writings*. The lines "Her body a system of emotions and triggers lost. Every hair lost in the bath. Every dead cell rubbed off on a towel" in the *Professional Model*, 1933 section are from chapter 1 of Michael Ondaatje's *Coming through Slaughter*. The lines "sitting on silk and satin coverlets spread across the floor" and "Your eyes got sore looking at the dazzling whiteness of the oval or round-shaped pearls which hung in ropes around their necks, sending their glittering rays around edges of the room" in the *Child Wife*, March 1936 section are also from Vivan Sundaram's *Amrita Sher-Gil*. In the *Study for Composition, 1936* section, the lines are also from Vivan Sundaram's *Amrita Sher-Gil*:

> The point being that good art always tends towards simplification. That is to say, it only considers the essentials of a form. The stress is invariably laid on the textural and structural beauty of the work instead of the subject depicted. Form is never imitated, it is always interpreted. The aim of art being the deprival of aesthetic emotion from abstract beauty, the vitality

of line, form, color and design, as opposed to the pleasure derived from the prettiness of the object depicted in the picture. Left to their own initiative, the great majority of people lapse into the common error of trying to discover in pictures emotional pegs on which to hang their feelings and imagine what they derive from the process is synonymous with the real aesthetic emotion the initiated derive from the contemplation of sheer pictorial beauty.

Lastly, in the *Woman in Red, 1936* section, the lines "My red children had, but never got" are an interpolation of the lines "You remember the children you got that you did not get" from Gwendolyn Brooks's poem "The Mother" in *A Street in Bronzeville* (1945) section of *Blacks* by Gwendolyn Brooks, edited by Third World Press.

Frame Eleven uses the lines "At the close of foreday morning" from *Journal of a Homecoming/Cahier d'un retour au pays natal* by Aimé Césaire, translated by N. Gregson Davis.

Paean to Chikumbi is after Lorine Niedecker's poem "Paean to Place" from *Lorine Niedecker: Collected Works* edited by Jenny Penberthy.

At David Livingstone's Statue uses the lines "I come neither as saint nor sinner. I am prepared to go anywhere, provided it be forward" from the Charles Rivers Editors' *Dr. David Livingstone: The Life and Legacy of the Victorian Era's Most Famous Explorer and Pioneer*. It also uses the lines "The recordings of his barren solitude heated by poisonous winds, his treks through the wild jungles infested by snakes and only roamed over by a few scattered tribes of untameable barbarians" from M. NourbeSe Philip's *Looking for Livingstone: An Odyssey of Silence*.

Frame Twelve uses lines from:

Ariana Reines, "I Want You to Inject My Face with Botulism," *The Cow*
    "The luster of something"

Ariana Reines, "Knocker," *The Cow*
    "Apertures"

Ariana Reines, "Section Two: Save the World," *The Cow*
"Everything has form"

César Vallejo, "Trilce: XLVIII," *The Complete Poetry*, translated by Clayton
Eshleman
"Unleashing arduous, scintillating silences"

Edward Hirsch, "A Chinese Vase," *The Living Fire: New and Selected Poems*
"To forget the impossible weight of being human"

Edward Hirsch, "Dusk," *The Living Fire: New and Selected Poems*
"Dusk with its desperate colors of erasure"

Edward Hirsch, "Four A. M.," *The Living Fire: New and Selected Poems*
"The hollow, unearthly hour of night"
"The very dirge"

Edward Hirsch, "Heinrich Heine," *The Living Fire: New and Selected Poems*
"I am an addict of the human comedy"

Edward Hirsch, "Indian Summer," *The Living Fire: New and Selected Poems*
"I've imagined it all"

Edward Hirsch, "Porter," *The Living Fire: New and Selected Poems*
"This is my other heritage"

Gerald Barrax, "Efficiency Apartment," *From a Person Sitting in Darkness: New and
Selected Poems*
"And the stretched out ends our lives make"

Marilyn Nelson, "Cover Photograph," *The Fields of Praise: New and Selected Poems*
"The lullaby of shadows"

Melvin B. Tolson, "Rendezvous with America," *Harlem Gallery and Other Poems*,
edited by Raymond Nelson.
"The flavors of tongues"

Wanda Coleman, "The Essential Flavors of the Finite," *The World Falls Away*
"To settle into the flesh of our futures"

Dear Suzanne uses the lines "it [is] imperatively the time for dissent, and essentially for dissident thinking" and "to grasp beyond the known limits of civilizations" from, and is after, *The Great Camouflage: Writings of Dissent (1941–1945)* by Suzanne Césaire, translated by Keith L. Walker, and edited by Daniel Maximin. In addition, it uses the lines "a cruel aggressive pleasure, a settling of accounts with colonial ugliness (sadism) and also a pleasure of experiencing the wounds received in order to be better able to proclaim the legitimacy of the cause (masochism)"; "It alone conceives of worlds in which man, if he lived in them, would cease to feel himself a stranger"; and "to transport us into an extraordinary world: the land of the marvellous" from *Refusal of the Shadow: Surrealism and the Caribbean* translated and edited by Michael Richardson and Krzysztof Fijalkowski. It also uses the line "To be present in history down to the marrow" from Édouard Glissant's poem "Lavas" in the collection *Riveted Blood* from *The Collected Poems of Édouard Glissant*, translated by Jeff Humphries.

ACKNOWLEDGMENTS

Thank you to the following journals where some of the poems, sometimes in earlier forms, in this book have or will be published: *New England Review*: "Lester Leaps In"; *Lolwe*: "Getting Lost with Hayao Miyazaki and Satoshi Kon" and "Pastoral"; *Birdfeast*: "That Same Pain, That Same Pleasure"; *The Paris Review*: "Frame Six" and "At David Livingstone's Statue"; *Hampden-Sydney Poetry Review*: "The Code of Hammurabi"; *Boston Review*: As winners of the 2020 Boston Review Annual Poetry Contest judged by Alexis Pauline Gumbs, "Notes toward a Biography of Henry Tayali" and "Djibril Diop Mambéty's Scene Descriptions" appeared in the *Ancestors* winter arts issue.

Zikomo (thank you) and madaliso (blessings) to my various tribes. I offer my infinite gratitude to my teachers, scholars, translators, friends, and peers of all schools, institutional and not, that have blessed me and this work.

An especial thank you to the African Poetry Book Fund, home of the Sillerman First Book Prize for African Poetry, and the University of Nebraska Press team. Immense gratitude goes to Kwame Dawes, Chris Abani, Gabeba Baderoon, Phillippa Yaa De Villiers, Bernardine Evaristo, Aracelis Girmay, John Keene, Matthew Shenoda, Ashley Strosnider, Joeth Zucco, Nathan Putens, Tish Fobben, Rosemary Sekora, Andrea Shahan, Johnson Uwandinma for letting us use your beautiful painting as the cover, and Courtney Ochsner.

And infinite thank-yous to my blurbers, whose work and personas continue to remain the most indelible mark on my being. Thank you to M. NourbeSe Philip, Rigoberto González, John Keene, and A. Van Jordan.

Thank you to my Rutgers and Middlebury teachers and guides: A. Van Jordan, Brenda Shaughnessy, Cathy Park Hong, Rigoberto González, John Keene, Melissa Hartland, William Hart, Christopher Shaw, Karin Gottshall, Alvin Henry, Jessyka Finley, Ann Hanson, and Hector Vila.

An especial thank-you to my love, Johanna Tesfaye. You are the one constant who has rewritten, edited, and overseen the completion of this book with me. Here is to your most keen eye; your sublime, supreme, and most high love; and the countless etcetaras of why I love you.

For your supreme editorship, much gratitude to John McCarthy, Ebenezer Agu, Xandria Phillips, and Aaron Coleman.

For your conversations regarding the craft of it all, the love for it all, the long game of it all, the necessity of it all, the politics of it all, and the kinship of it all, thank you for your sustenance Simeon Marsalis, Dimitri Reyes, Antonio López, Musa Syeed for introducing me to Andrei Tarkovsky's *Sculpting in Time*, Phillip B. Williams, I. S. Jones, and Joël Díaz.

To my kinfolk who were my first witnesses. Strength and guidance to us all. Jason Leehow, Davi Miller, Ben Harker, Osaze Riley, Tamir Williams, Ruchita Chandrashekar, Ariana Jordan, and Emeka Nnaubo.

A special thank-you to Jamilyn Bailey who introduced me to Rilke's *Letters to a Young Poet*. I hope this work is evidence that I have not forgotten your kindness.

For providing time, space, food of various material, and the economical means to keep this afloat, a thank-you to Jennifer Grotz and Michael Collier at the Bread Loaf Writers' Conference, Toi Derricotte and Cornelius Eady at Cave Canem, Greg Pardlo at the Callaloo Creative Writing Workshop in Barbados, Marita Golden, Clyde McElvene, and Deborah Heard at the Hurston/Wright Foundation.

I close with my blood. My grandmother Margaret Phiri and my mother, Maunda Phiri, for their courageous leap into the tumultuous unknown they turned into a paradise. Sacrifice feels like such an undermining word for what you have given. I owe an eternal debt—a labyrinth of thank-yous. To my brother, Nkhope Mphanza, and the spirit of my father, Harry Mphanza. Family, I hope I have honored this blood.

Gabriel Okara: Collected Poems
Gabriel Okara
Edited and with an introduction
by Brenda Marie Osbey

Sacrament of Bodies
Romeo Oriogun

The Kitchen-Dweller's Testimony
Ladan Osman
Foreword by Kwame Dawes

Fuchsia
Mahtem Shiferraw

Your Body Is War
Mahtem Shiferraw
Foreword by Kwame Dawes

In a Language That You Know
Len Verwey

Logotherapy
Mukoma Wa Ngugi

When the Wanderers Come Home
Patricia Jabbeh Wesley

Seven New Generation African Poets:
A Chapbook Box Set
Edited by Kwame Dawes
and Chris Abani
(Slapering Hol)

Eight New-Generation African Poets:
A Chapbook Box Set
Edited by Kwame Dawes
and Chris Abani
(Akashic Books)

New-Generation African Poets:
A Chapbook Box Set (Tatu)
Edited by Kwame Dawes
and Chris Abani
(Akashic Books)

New-Generation African Poets:
A Chapbook Box Set (Nne)
Edited by Kwame Dawes
and Chris Abani
(Akashic Books)

New-Generation African Poets:
A Chapbook Box Set (Tano)
Edited by Kwame Dawes
and Chris Abani
(Akashic Books)

To order or obtain more information on these or other University of
Nebraska Press titles, visit nebraskapress.unl.edu. For more information
about the African Poetry Book Series, visit africanpoetrybf.unl.edu.